In My DNA

In My DNA

By

Arthur Bloom

Arthurdbloom2@gmail.com

Printed in the United States of America

Library of Congress Data
ISBN 978-0-578-40902-3 (paperback)

Cover Designer: Cheryl Uyeda
Interior Design: Jason Pearce

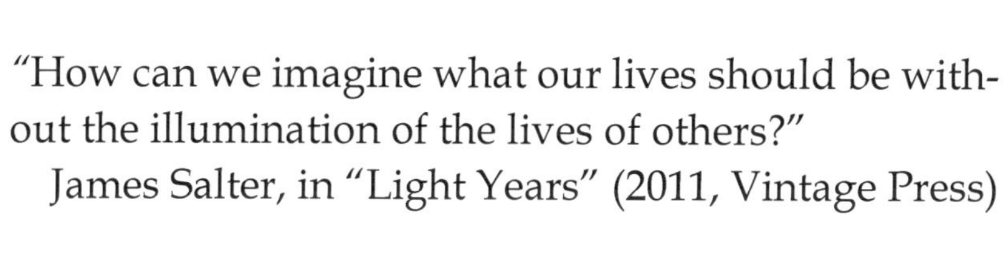

"How can we imagine what our lives should be without the illumination of the lives of others?"
James Salter, in "Light Years" (2011, Vintage Press)

For Deborah, my Love and Muse

Without whose spirit and joie de vivre
my life would not have been what it became
and this book could not have been written

Also by Arthur Bloom*

Tales of an American Émigré in Paris, Editions des Ecrivains, Paris, 2000 (Essays)

Citron's Sonata, Athena Press, London, 2007 (A Novel)

From Neighborhood to Manhood: *The Boys of Blue Hill Avenue*, Small Batch Books, Amherst, MA, 2011 (Biographical Essays)

Last Man Standing: Stories, Harvard Book Store/Amazon Press, Cambridge, MA, 2014 (Stories)

*In addition, Arthur Bloom has authored or edited nine medical books and published 121 original biomedical science research papers, primarily in genetics and environmental health.

Acknowledgments

I thank Philip Storey, poet, of Gloucester, for his incisive editorial help with the manuscript; Cheryl Uyeda, graphics designer of Los Angeles, for the excellent cover design; and Jerome Bender, attorney and friend, of New York City for his reading and comments on the text. Jean MacCluer, friend and colleague of San Antonio, sampled parts of the book prior to its publication and gave helpful feedback. My son Noah Bloom read and critiqued parts of the manuscript and gave the book its title. Daughter Michelle made insightful comments throughout this process.

I have tried to be faithful throughout to the truth but some names may have been changed inadvertently or purposefully, and some episodes herein described may have interpretations different from my own – for these differences I have to shrug my shoulders: I tried to be transparent. To my children Karen, Michelle, Robert and Noah, now all grown, and for their children yet to come, I apologize for any perceived invasions of privacy. My paramount concern throughout has been protection of my loved ones while delivering to them the essence of my life story.

Table of Contents

Introduction: The Fire

Smoke from the forest fire had begun approaching us that weekend, with ashes covering the windows of the car and the pungent odors of burning deciduous timber penetrating the air throughout the Tennessee mountain on which we then lived. The police were reassuring, however, telling us all that the fire was under control. We wanted to believe them and so we did.

This was the Great Smokey Mountain National Park, in Eastern Tennessee and we were thereby under the care of the National Park Service as well as the Gatlinburg Tennessee Police Department. Who were we to not follow their instructions?

On the Sunday night before the fateful Monday - 28 November 2016 - four black bears came to visit, a Momma bear and her three cubs. This was a family known to us over the year and a half we had lived in this cabin, because the bears, sometimes with Poppa Bear, had often visited. We had a rivulet that ran the length of our driveway, and these bears, along with families of wild turkeys, would often stop by to slake their thirst. I came to Tennessee to write a book, this book, and had come to relish the quiet this place in nature afforded me.

But this visit of the bears differed from those past: this time the Momma and cubs came brazenly onto our deck, and attempted to remove the cover of the hot tub, to get to the water. My wife and I and our two dogs watched them in awe from behind the tightly closed glass doors, the dogs recoiling as the bears stood tall. Eventually, the bears left, frustrated no doubt at their inability to get to the water.

But now, on Monday morning, the smoke was much closer than it had been even the evening before. It had this day enshrouded us in its cocoon, and we could smell the smoke from the burning trees inside the house.

Many moons ago, in December of 1960, when I was a young intern at Bellevue Hospital, the City summoned all its duly employed medical personnel to the Brooklyn Navy Yard where an aircraft carrier, the USS Constellation, was burning. The construction workers in the hold of the ship were brought out to the pier on which our ambulances and medical supplies were dispatched. I remember basically being asked to listen to the chests of these men, these heroes, whose flesh was singed by the fire. We were asked to pronounce dead those who were dead, and to send the others for oxygen and intravenous fluids so they might be saved. The image of the ship's welders and carpenters whose nasal passages and lungs were filled with smoke remained fixed in my mind as a reminder of the effects of smoke alone, the real killer so often in fires.

And thus, we called the Gatlinburg Police Department repeatedly that Monday morning to be sure the fire would ultimately leave us be. We were repeatedly told to stay at home, behind closed doors, "things are under control."

As the morning wore on, however, the smoke got worse inside and without the house, and by early afternoon, as I looked out the windows, I could see the leaves from a late fall season being blown about increasingly – the winds were obviously increasing and the visibility outside was decreasing. Despite the official words of those supposedly our protectors, I said it was time to go down the sole mountain road and out of harm's way.

We gathered our passports as well as our minipoodle Rico and our English bulldog Jacques, got in the Malibu, and drove down the mountain road and west towards a clear sky some forty miles distant. We literally had only the clothes on our backs; left the Nikon, the Bose, and the iPad, and were happy, relieved, to get away alive, which at least fourteen others did not. One fallen tree or telephone pole across that road would have blocked us as it later did many others, as the fire spread over the next four or five hours. Our house was incinerated, we later learned, along with some two thousand other homes and buildings on our mountain and the surrounding area. The fire had descended directly onto our home from the mountain top.

This book was written, then, in two parts: Chapters One to Ten cover my life from the early days in Dorchester, Massachusetts, through my years in Hiroshima and my professorship at Columbia, while Chapters Eleven through Fourteen cover my life that followed New York, the Paris years, until my return more recently to Massachusetts. The tone may well be different – the Gatlinburg fire left me at more than 80 years of age with few clothes and little else. My Nikon and most of its Memory Cards, covering much of our life in Paris had been incinerated, along with my sound system, iPad, fountain pen – I loved the feel of that pen, a proper fountain pen, my shaving brush and razor, and so many smaller items that one takes for granted especially after a "certain age."

So, the reader may detect my sadness, a change in world view, in the last part of the book. I cannot change the emotional impact of an event so catastrophic as the destruction of a life by a forest fire. I can only beg the reader's forbearance.

• • •

For a geneticist, which I was for most of my professional life, the word "evolution" implies evolution of a species; but for me as a writer, and in particular as the writer of this my life story, evolution has also and more importantly to do with the evolution of my being. The individual, in particular this individual, was not, and is not a fixed, immutable personality, with set goals, established and fixed ways of being in the world. My story illustrates that with a certain kind of freedom, the freedom that comes with change, voluntary or imposed, the seeming immutable is in fact mutable. Sometime in the summer of 1983, I had a dream, a nightmare really: I was in a closed room on campus with a group of my colleagues from Columbia University, having drinks. We were standing about, sipping, chatting, when I noticed that the radiator valves were suddenly hissing and the gas emanating from the radiators was not the usual steam but rather some malodorous gas. One by one my colleagues began slipping to the floor, dying, gasping for air. I began banging on the door to the room, shouting in a panic,"Let me out." Trapped, I awoke in near hysteria.......

• • •

I had long wished to become a professor – a full professor – at a major university and I had succeeded at age 40, having been recruited by Columbia from the University of Michigan where I was an Associate Professor of Human Genetics and of Pediatrics. I had all the trappings of academic achievement: a clinic of my own, a laboratory of my own, and I served on many prestigious committees at the medical school, including the Admissions Committee, as well as nationally and internationally. I was invited widely to speak at medical genetic conferences, within the State and outside it, from Kalamazoo to Palo Alto and Edinburgh. I appeared on television on Detroit stations, to discuss "inherited criminality," and then on New York channels, including the PBS News Hour with McNeill and Lehrer, to discuss the potential genetic effects at Three Mile Island.

And yet, and yet...While all very interesting and exciting, I came to feel that I lacked something in my life. One day when we had spent the better part of thirty minutes at a Columbia University Department of Pediatrics Faculty Meeting discussing the state of the stairwells at our (Babies) Hospital – too dirty – and how to remedy the situation, I went to a solo lunch across the street at the local Washington Heights Cuban-Chinese Restaurant I frequented and tried to think it all through. Wherein lay my sense of dissatisfaction? Back in Boston Days when I was growing up, and again at Harvard College in my Undergraduate Days, I had dreamed of not only becoming a doctor but also of spending my days writing, fiction, non-fiction, whatever. And so I decided to start taking courses in the Writing Program on the Main Campus at Columbia to see if that would ease my sense of malaise. I followed that first course on fiction writing with a summer's course at the New York State Writer's Institute, which had been started by Frank McCourt in Albany, McCourt whose Irish roots and writing talents I very much appreciated.

And so, slowly, it came to pass that I became more a person of literature and the arts than a man of science. By the time I arrived some years later in Paris to develop a program devoted to studying the environmental health effects of the Soviet contamination of Eastern Europe, I was well on my way mentally to giving up medicine and genetical science in favor of a life of the literary mind. I came to sit in our apartment in the 16th arrondissement in Paris, looking out the window at the sole tree in the courtyard and across the courtyard at the neighbors who variously piqued my curiosity, for their attire, their furnishings, their smoking habits. The end result was my first book of essays devoted to the upsy-daisy life of an American émigré in Paris. From that point, I increasingly focused my work life, and my habits, on books: reading and writing them.

In Paris that shift was easy, relatively, as nothing and no one in France is valued as highly as a writer. People listen to writers talking endlessly on the television at all hours of the night and day, and people race to the *librairies* (bookstores) in their neighborhoods to be among the first to buy the latest prize-winning books of the year - the Goncourt, the Prix Femina, et alia. In Paris cafes writers *like me* can sit for hours over a small espresso, typing silently on their PC's, while the men in suits conduct the City's business. And so I evolved into someone who reads and writes all the time.

In France it is generally not believed that writers can be taught the art of writing - one either has the ability or one does not. This differs from the U.S. where courses and workshops abound. In any case on my return to the U.S. after many years in France I determined that I would remain faithful to my new way and write as a way of life, giving up medicine and science -and the income they provided - for a gentler way of being in the world. This book is one result of that decision.

Back in the States, I went from Vermont to Massachusetts and then to Appalachia in Eastern Tennessee. I have wandered these past five years, trying to find my place in my own country, a place, where I felt at home. My search has progressed, especially since the forest fire, and I am back to my roots now in Massachusetts, by the sea.

1

Family Origins and Troubles

Boston

Like most everyone in this country I am of immigrant stock. Both sets of grandparents originated from parts of Poland and White Russia where Jews were persecuted during harsh *progroms,* where males were involuntarily conscripted into the service of the Tsar, and where most of my forefathers lived in *shtells,* little villages, where they farmed and controlled their local lives to a greater or lesser extent. My people also lived, of course, in the major cities of Europe, in ghettoes too often, but sometimes, under more enlightened regimes, integrated into the larger society. My grandparents were not integrated there - or here for that matter - and were nothing but fodder for the Tsar's *m'shigas,* his craziness.

Once the family at least partially succeeded in the New World, in Boston to be precise, most moved from Malden and Chelsea to the north into the newer in-city Boston Jewish ghettoes of Dorchester and Roxbury, where the elite met. Dorchester and Roxbury were thought, at one time, to be rising suburbs of the city: transportation into Boston was facilitated by the MTA, the transport system that criss-crossed the city and allowed access to jobs from all points; and housing was either in reasonably-priced apartments in often rundown three story, six family New England houses or in free-standing, modest single-family homes, on tiny lots, for the somewhat more affluent. All, however, were part of working class Boston.

Growing up, I lived in several such New England apartments, because my parents, whose marriage was a struggle, had little money. My father was both a womanizer, I later learned, and a gambler, though he was also what everyone called a "nice guy." I remember him as a gentle, handsome man, who stirred my interest in baseball, especially in the Boston Braves, then still a power in Boston under its owner the construction guy Lou Perini. My father himself had been a member of the Braves Knothole Gang – entitling him to free admission to Braves' games from time to time, a gesture Perini made to the Boston underclass - when my father himself was a youngster growing up in Boston. He was always quick to point out that he was in attendance in 1920 when the Braves and the Brooklyn Dodgers played the longest baseball game in Major League history, to then or now, some 26 innings. No lights in those days, so they played to a 1-1 tie, in an amazing three hours and fifty minutes, until darkness set in.

I grew up, then, under my father's tutelage, a strong National League fan, and my childhood moods changed with the fortunes of the Braves during my earliest youth, in World War II. The Braves were irresistible and featured Tommy Holmes, the singles hitter who won batting titles; Chuck Workman, the left fielder who struck out or homcred, it was always a crapshoot; the pitchers Warren Spahn, greatest lefty I ever saw - what a curve he threw! - and Johnny Sain, with a terrific fastball and curve. Once Lew Burdette joined them they would go on to win the National League pennant in 1948, after the War. By then they had racist Alvin Dark at shortstop, bespectacled Earl Torgeson in the infield, and consistent Danny Litwhiler pairing with Holmes in the outfield.

Thus, when the Braves were moved (1953) by (the bastard) Perini to Milwaukee - Milwaukee, for Christ's sake! - it was an act of high treason and my devotion to them and the National League was finished forever. And yet I could not simply switch to support the Red Sox of Boston - that would have been a treasonous act, despite the great Ted Williams, the brilliant infielders Johnny Pesky and Bobby Doerr and that other Dimaggio, the Little Professor Dominic, out in center field. And so I turn-coated to the Yankees of New York, a city and team I would come to relish for a lifetime.

Dad went off to the War in 1943, drafted even though he had a wife and son to support - lowest priority in the draft were sole-support guys who were married with kids. Up at the Great Lakes Naval Training Center he jumped some 100 feet into a pool - as he would have had to do were he on a sinking battleship - and became a serious hero to me. Stationed at the Quonset Point Rhode Island Naval base during the War, he was scheduled to ship out to the European

Theater as a radioman first class, after drawing the short straw among the radiomen then stationed at Quonset Point.

My father was a "short straw" guy much of his life. He bribed a younger, unattached seaman to go in his stead – the Navy cared not who went so long as someone with that skill filled the slot - so Dad spent the rest of the War coming home to Dorchester from nearby Rhode Island two or three weekends a month. Not that that helped his relationship with my mother, not at all; but at least he and I could take in a Braves game from time to time, so it mattered to me. He smoked his Chesterfield cigarettes at a great rate, and nibbled endlessly on Milky Ways.

When the War ended, our troubles really began. My father was the youngest of five Bloom siblings – there was Jake, Macey, Harry, Ida, and dad – and he was ill-equipped, except physically, for the requirements of marriage. He was a handsome man, about 5′8″, and had a really pleasant disposition about him so everyone liked him. But, he had been babied by everyone in his family, especially his mother, and he had little sense of "responsibility," that was the party line. The fun-loving side of him put him into direct conflict with my mother who was herself the oldest of six siblings, two of whom died very early - one of diphtheria, one of scarlet fever - and she was the power, next to her own mother, among her surviving sibs: Fanny, Sam, and Edward Israel. My mother was a dynamo, with strong ideas on how things should be done, and she was the born boss of us all – second only to my grandmother, her mother Annie, who was stronger still. Dad was simply overpowered by them both and so he reverted to bad habits like gambling and womanizing, to feel a bit better about himself, I suppose, I don't really know. We had had to move in with grandmother and grandfather over on Dyer Street towards Codman Square, in Saint Matthews Parish, during the War when dad was drafted, to make ends meet, so we were one complex family with which dad had to contend on his weekends and then on his permanent return from Quonset Point in 1945.

During his Navy time, when I was less than ten, I had come home from school one day to find mother convulsed in tears and grandmother in a rage. I was told that someone had broken in and stolen our linens, silverware, and China ware. Later in life - not much later- I learned that dad had hocked the stuff to help pay off the bookies who were threatening to break his legs if he did not make good on his accumulating gambling debts.

Mother and dad kept up the charade of a marriage a few more years as divorce in those days was rare and very traumatic - plus they tried to protect me and themselves from the notoriety (and shame) that would go with a divorce.

When my father emerged from this man's Navy in 1945, he resolved to become an independent businessman, compliments of the GI Bill which entitled him to loans to establish his own company, which he did on lower Washington Street in downtown Boston. He opened a wholesale paper company, the Bradford Paper Company, for which he had trained under Uncles Jake and Macey before going off to war. Turned out, he used the Government's money not only to set up his company - which I often visited on Saturdays, after Shabbat services - but mainly to play the ponies and dogs. I was proud, I remember, to go to "our" company for my visits and he enjoyed having me around for a few hours most weeks while I treasured our time together in his business. I did not want to learn the business, mind you, I just wanted to be around him.

Ultimately, though, he used a lot of that GI Bill money plus other funds borrowed from family and friends – that was the real deal breaker - to bet on dog races at Wonderland out in Revere, and on horse races at Suffolk Downs and all around New England. Of course he mainly lost and got us far into debt – "us" because the family, especially mother, had to assume his obligations, morally if not legally. That post-War behavior, along with the long history of gambling, resulted in an acrimonious divorce when I was 13, about to be *bar mitzvahed.*

A debate raged within the family as to how the bar mitzvah should be handled. The custom then as now was a celebratory meal either right after the service in *shul* or a dinner in the evening, with dancing, lots of kosher, of course, food, preferably in a private club rented for the occasion, such as the Aperion Plaza over on Warren Street in nearby Roxbury. We had neither the money for such a fete nor the inclination. Mother, who was footing the bill for all this, decided on a buffet lunch at the social hall of the Temple where I had been studying my *Haftorah* portion and preparing my English-language speech in praise of God.

I had always been a good student and was certainly one at the Hebrew School I attended five days a week, in preparation for my readings at my Bar Mitzvah. Reb Myer Goldman, my main teacher, was a chicken slaughterer by day, and a Hebrew teacher – 4 p.m.to 7 p.m. - after his days at the slaughter house, Mondays through Fridays plus Sunday mornings. He would roar at me, us, whenever we made a mistake - nothing personal, it was his way - so I made fewer and fewer as the October bar mitzvah date neared. Goldman had a ruler which he wielded with a certain fury for the misbegotten, so I was motivated.

The Torah reading was, with the *Haftorah* portion, a prescribed section of the Five Books; but the English speech was mine for the drafting with a lot of help from the *kibitzers*, as you might imagine. We - Mother, the Rabbi and I - fought over one key phrase in the speech, which summed up the issue of my life to that point in time: The speech was to address family and friends, as well as the Rabbi and God, but the Family was in tumult over the divorce, so when I wrote, "Dearly Beloved Rabbi, Parents, Relatives, and Friends…." my mother would have none of it, insisting, with a vehemence I could not abide yet could not overcome - at age 13 or ever - that the proper phrase was, "Dearly Beloved Rabbi, Parent, Relatives and Friends….." Unknown to me, initially, my father was not even being invited to the Service, and certainly not the luncheon, let alone was he asked to do a reading as was customary for the fathers of Bar Mitzvah boys, including the fathers of all my friends. I was chagrined and often in tears, mostly internal, at all this, but there was no arguing with mother, or grandmother, they had been publicly disgraced by dad and he was persona non-grata.

In fact, he did show up at the Synagogue, sat in the back row, as I read "Parent", but did not come to the luncheon that followed, as mother was unforgiving. I just wanted to be through with the pain of it all, and after the Bar Mitzvah

I finished my sixth and last year of Hebrew School, deciding not to go on to the Hebrew High School which at least several classmates did and which I wanted to do but was urged to choose between the Boston Latin School or the after-school Hebrew High School since mother did not wish me to "take on too much." I am not sure why but she always seemed to worry, needlessly I felt, about my fragility. Among my Hebrew School classmates who did go on to the Hebrew High School was the beautiful daughter of Rabbi Perl with whom I was in love at the time. I would have done many years of study to be near her on a daily basis.

Dad would occasionally wait outside the Beth Hillel Hebrew School on Morton Street to walk me home - that was awkward but it was good just to see him - and we would regularly go candlepin bowling at the lanes at South Station on Saturday afternoons - he was a good bowler, I remember that, and a good athlete, generally. But, the bookies were after him and he had to make himself scarce. When my 14th birthday came around the next year, he called to wish me a Happy Birthday - he and mother had been battling all year over alimony and child support, but he had no job, and no money and she had to resume secretarial work to start paying off his debts which ran into many thousands of dollars. Mother insisted I hang up the birthday phone, which I duly did - and that was the last time I ever heard from him.

Soon thereafter she had him thrown into the Charles Street Jail for non-payment, and even now I cannot walk past or into the hotel that prison has become - ironically the Liberty Hotel, a fancy boutique hotel and disco joint - without a big tear erupting in my heart.

My father moved to Rhode Island to escape his creditors (and probably my mother and her bastard lawyer); and while his brothers speculated that he may have had a second family there, I know nothing of it. I do know by word from Uncle Macey that my father gained a tremendous amount of weight, became hypertensive, had a massive stroke at age 63, and was dead at 65.

I was by then a professor living in the Midwest. Mother knew of his death, but told me only after he was buried, up in Boston at the West Roxbury Cemetery with his parents Sam and Bessie, and his sister Ida Barg. The U.S. Navy placed a plaque on his grave, which I have visited on several occasions – when I was up to the challenge, asking his forgiveness for my failure to hunt him up, and at the same time cursing him for abandoning me though truth is I mostly blamed mother for his absence.

He had in his wallet at the time of his death, in addition to his Social Security card, a picture of me as I was when a member at age 14 of the Frank V. Thompson Junior High School Marching Band, in my uniform.

My inability to cast aside the domination of my mother then and later has been a curse. She was of course totally devoted to my well-being, she claimed, but I have often thought maybe it was her own well-being that motivated her. Probably and understandably a bit of both. She claimed she did not want dad's pernicious influence to cost me my life – she would even panic when I showed interest in playing a little poker with my pals – demotivate me from going to college, make me a Gamblin' Man, too. My father died not knowing me and I shall die not having known him.

2

Boston Latin – Sumus Primi

The Boston Public School System had magnet high schools and I was blessed to get into one of the best of them, the Boys Latin School (BLS) down on Avenue Louis Pasteur in the Fenway area. The Latin School drew in "the better boys of Boston," as one of our Masters used to say, and it was regarded as The School to prepare you for college, especially for Harvard College. You had to take exams to get in, unless your grades in junior high - or elementary school if you chose to enter for the 7th grade (Class VI) - were high enough. I had somehow emerged from the trauma of the divorce in my junior high years with super grades and so I easily qualified for entrance. I was intent on going despite some cautionary advice to Mother and me about the School maybe being "too hard at this time in my life".

After I received my second month's Latin Grade, however, a clear flunk, a 50 with 60 being passing, I felt I was one step from the BLS exit door. I was blessed to have an uncle who had studied Latin at BLS and he agreed to take me on, to drill me in ablatives and datives and declensions, so I was given a helping hand. Problem was I had the toughest Latin Master in the whole school, one Doc Roche. Doc gave us a quiz a week, graded it out of five points, and he deducted one point for each mistake – so two mistakes in the Latin declension of a verb and you were already at 3/5 or 60%, a bare pass. I had trouble mastering the nouns and verbs and Uncle Sam was a pro at grinding me on these. Before the next month was out, I had raised my monthly grade to the highest anyone got all year, an 84 – I had gotten four 4/5's, and Doc Roche gave me a few points just for showing up. Of course, there was no charity in his heart as an 85 was equivalent to an A, and no one was to get an 85 or higher all year.

I was working after school at the New England Wholesale Drug Company near my house, stocking shelves and sweeping up, two to three hours a day, and fighting off the advances of the gay and aggressive store manager named Oscar. Oscar obviously liked young boys, but I needed the money, so I had to keep that job, as well as my integrity, and I was not at all interested. Fortunately, Oscar backed off and we were eventually fine. But that job meant I had to study until two or three a.m. every night to do well at BLS, which I always did after that near catastrophe in Latin.

The tradition of excellence at that school made us all proud to be there – 200 left in my class after the fifteen dropouts of that first year. I, in fact, became a very good Latin Scholar, advanced quickly from Caesar to Cicero to Virgil in the next couple of years, never got another failing grade, and finished highly ranked in my class.

But, Harvard, well, that was another story. We had no

money and mother was petrified I would be unable to go to college at all, let alone Harvard. Of course, by saving our shekels, working very hard after school and summers while she ran the Boston version of the Zionist House down on Commonwealth Avenue, we might get me through Boston University or Northeastern which were less expensive. I had other ideas, however: the BLS influence, and was desperate to get to Harvard.

The story was that certain Masters - not Teachers, but Masters - at BLS had strong contacts at Harvard and Harvard looked to the BLS to make its "contribution" to the Boston Community. One of the more influential Masters in this regard was Max Levine, who ran the French Club at BLS - a Mr. Chips-type of teacher-Master, a man who devoted his life to "his boys". (Later, once I began writing non-science books, I based The Old Man of "The Old Man and The Boy" story - see *Last Man Standing: Stories* (2014) - on Max Levine and the life I imagined for him.)

I loved French even then and was a stellar French student. Plus, and this mattered to Max, I was a leader among my classmates: Secretary of the BLS Chapter of the National Honor Society, elected president of the German Club, and later of the Latin Club - the irony was not lost on me! - and I just missed being elected Class Secretary. The Irish guys from Southie and Jamaica Plain outnumbered the Jewish guys from Dorchester and Roxbury, so Quinlan beat Bloom in the run-off. When time came the end of junior year to name the President of the French Club, a position appointed by Max, who left nil to chance, and perhaps the most prestigious club presidency at BLS, he named me to my amazement. It was a great honor, because the President of Max's French Club had a fast track into Harvard on a scholarship.

The BLS experience went well beyond, but was firmly based in, grades and extra-curriculars. But it was so much more than that: It gave "the boys" of Boston a sense of togetherness, in dealing successfully for the most part with a system of education in the form of masters who were demanding achievement-wise in the classroom and very tough verbally on us in class. Further, it gave us a sense of pride in who we were, where we came from, where we might be going. At Assembly the eyes looked up inevitably at the few names etched on the walls: Cotton Mather, Class of 1689; Benjamin Franklin, Class of 1714; Samuel Adams, Class of 1729; Charles Bulfinch, Class of 1770; Ralph Waldo Emerson, 1812; Charles Eliot, 1844; and a few others, with one blank space still available at that time - the 1950's - and that was said to be reserved for George Santayana, Class of 1878, a philosopher and writer who was still alive and living in Rome. Santayana's death seemed to be eagerly awaited at BLS so his name could be etched in stone. (He died finally in 1952, the year we graduated, and his name, as promised, was duly added to the frieze.)

My family was generally supportive of my successes but there was grumbling in the background about my ability, given the absence of a dad, to proceed in a full-throated way to lead my life. The family seemed worried as to how I would turn out: be a Gamblin' Man like my father, or a Professional Man, as Mother and Grandmother wished for me and I for myself. Grandmother, in particular, was pushing me mercilessly in the direction of Medicine, and she could be tough.

There were helping hands all along the way, beginning in Class IV when Uncle Sam turned me into that Latin Scholar, through Classes III when I solidified my reputation and academic accomplishments, to Class II when I actually went to Summer School to study Cicero (!) so I could move from IIB to Class IIA where those who started BLS – and Latin - in the seventh grade were grouped. When I did officially get in to Harvard with a scholarship, loan and job waiting for me, in April of my Class I (senior) year, my scholar Uncle, Edward Israel, who was Class of '42 at Harvard, said, "I didn't know you were that smart". I came eventually to see that while no one discouraged my dreams, while the family was proud of me, it was mainly my mother and grandmother whose appreciation of my success was unqualified – the others were waiting to see what would become of me, waiting with a bit of anxiety and some skepticism, as they were competitive with mother and were accustomed to seeing their sister in a downtrodden position vis-à-vis themselves. Anyway, they loved me and my assumption of that was lifelong.

Meanwhile, there was a whole side of my birth family – my father's side – that had, because of the divorce, been cut from my life. It was a different kind of family but important in my earlier formative years when mother and father were still together. Uncle Jake was the owner of a wholesale paper company, and Uncle Macey worked with him for many years until he set off on his own. They were two marvelous characters, with a zest for life. They told stories, had a bit of fun, and when Aunt Sarah died of Parkinson's and Jake was alone, his three kids grown, Jake would date my mother, though she complained he was always a bit "tight" with the money and was hesitant to spend it though he surely had it. Jake's older son Larry was in the War, and while he had a terrible stammer, he was a decent chap, easy to like. I was about the same age as the younger sister Carol and she was one of my first loves – in theory, of course, one dared not marry a first cousin, it was against the Law. Macey was the best of the lot. He genuinely liked my father and me, and was, with his wife Evelyn and their talented artsy son Don, who was a cartoonist before becoming a painter and teacher of art, a joyful presence at our very occasional Bloom Family get-togethers.

I recently learned that Cousin Don went on to have a distinguished career, first as a cartoonist and later as an artist who experimented with color. He won Fulbrights and spent time in Europe before settling in as the head of an arts program at a high school in New Jersey, all the while building his reputation as a serious painter. I missed the pleasure of knowing him as an adult when the divorce split the Bloom Family off from mother and me.

But the Bloom I adored most at the time was Harry's boy Sonny. Harry himself was a bit of a rebel, marrying Irish Catholic Ellis at a time when marrying outside the faith was a serious sin. Ellis and Uncle Harry lived in a small apartment in Savin Hill over in South Boston, not a place we Jews generally went. But mother especially got on well with Ellis, and I worshipped Sonny, who was about eight years older than me, so it was fun to see and spend an occasional Sunday afternoon with them.

Sonny played the trombone and would practice all the time, it seemed to me, and as I was starting then on the bugle he was a musical inspiration. More importantly, Sonny built model airplanes out of balsa wood, and he knew and could recognize all the American, British and German fighter planes, from the P-51 Lightning and the Spitfire to the Messerschmidt – Sonny was fixated on aviation. In 1942 Sonny turned 18 – I was eight - and he immediately enlisted in the U.S. Air Corps. He became a first-rate pilot, flew off of the aircraft carrier the U.S.S. Hornet and later flew with General Claire Chenault's Flying Tigers over the Himalayas to supply the Chinese in their war with the Japanese. I worried about Sonny, and about my Uncle Sam who had landed at Normandy, and of course I worried a bit about my father, though I knew where he was. We just never knew when he would be shipped out.

I lost touch with all of these Blooms when my parents divorced. Partially it was in the nature of things for family and friends to take sides and partially it was a rigid division of life insisted on by mother, who really wanted nil to do with her "in-laws". But, for me, it added to my sadness to lose these close-in relatives. But, such was the hand I was given. I accepted it and lived my young life, nonetheless, with a certain vigor.

Another high school experience I had in South Boston had to do with a relationship I developed in an odd way. Over at Grandmother's on Dyer Street where we lived we had a party line. One Saturday night – it is like yesterday – I picked up the phone and could not get a dial tone. A young female voice kept asking was anyone on the line, could she have the line to make a call. I was then at the beginning of my flirtatious teenage years. I refused to relinquish the line, and so, in desperation, Isabel, accompanied by her younger sister Nancy, began to answer my questions, and I hers.

Isabel lived with her parents and sister on Mount Vernon Street - not THE Mt. Vernon Street on Beacon Hill but the Mt. Vernon Street in South Boston. Isabel's father worked for the Boston Edison and her mom was a homemaker, as it was colloquially called in those days. She and her family lived in Saint Margaret's Parish in Southie and she attended the Monsignor Ryan Memorial High School – now closed. We arranged to meet at a movie theater in Downtown Boston, and I was very nervous about this as Jews and Catholics did not mix in an amorous way – Grandmother would have killed me had she known. Anyway, Isabel and I liked each other, this tall, blond, upbeat Catholic girl from Southie and the Jewish kid from Boston Latin, *d'origine* Codman Square in Dorchester.

Our illicit, if innocent, get togethers were seriously challenged by Isabel's father who hated Jews with a passion. One Friday evening I was invited upstairs at 15 Mount Vernon by Isabel with permission of her mother – her father was presumably off at the local tavern spending his weekly paycheck. But he came home, saw me sitting at the kitchen table with Isabel, Nancy and his wife, so he grabbed a knife and chased me down the block, swearing as we both ran that, "no kike is going to date my daughter or sit in my kitchen." I escaped, if barely, and thereafter Isabel and I avoided our respective family living spaces, though we continued to see one another on the sly, despite her father and my grandmother, who knew from nothing but might have also grabbed a knife and chased Isabel down the street had she but known. That may be hyperbole concerning my Grandmother, but is an accurate description of her likely emotional response to her grandson dating a Catholic girl. (Note: When in later years I actually married a Catholic woman, I was blessed in that her name was "Schwarz", albeit without a "t".)

I continued to see Isabel even into the early years of Harvard and later on once in New York when I was at medical school and she was in town with Nancy for a weekend.

Noted: with only a rare communique between us from then on, I was nonetheless saddened to read of Isabel's recent death from cancer, leaving behind three children and grandchildren, no longer in South Boston but farther south in Weymouth to which she and her husband had moved in recent years. Her obituary had a picture of her, gray haired not blond, but with the same winning smile with which she enchanted the Jewish boy from Dorchester some 55 years earlier.

3

The Harvard Years – Veritas: The Deal Is Sealed

Cambridge

Between the Latin School and my ticket of admission to Harvard, I knew who I was and where I was going – to some extent. Who could demand more than that at age 18? But, when a young man arrives at Harvard, his world mutates from Day One. Harvard is that kind of place: even if one is not friendless and unknown upon arrival, as I was not, accompanied as I was by 98 others from the Latin School, the degree of difficulty in adjustment is huge, intellectually and socially.

First decision that had to be made was whether I could somehow find a way to live at the College. Given that Harvard was just across the Charles River from Boston, it was certainly possible for me to commute. Many, nay most, of my 98 Boston Latin School classmates who were going to Harvard with me were indeed commuting. Theirs was almost exclusively an economic decision. Mine though was born of desperation: I felt I had to leave the small one-bedroom apartment in Roxbury to which my mother and grandmother had moved. There was no place for me. Mother and grandmother Annie shared the one twin-bedded bedroom. When I was there, usually on Friday evenings, I was loved with chicken soup and chopped liver, my laundry folded, and their hugs of mother and grandmother. But I was assigned the couch in the living room adjacent to their bedroom, there being no place for an additional bed, a desk or a writing surface. Thus, the Harvard scholarship and loan I was given, plus my feeling that I would work and make a lot through my own efforts made me firmly committed to life in the Harvard Yard rather than on Seaver Street in Roxbury. I saw this as life or death for me, with the mice that frequented the walls of that apartment confirming my desperation. Still, leaving my two ladies was a wrench. Those Friday nights of freshman year lasted but a few months, and thereafter I spent most all my time at the College.

I worked the spring of senior year at BLS and on into the summer of '52 at the Harvard Medical School where I had applied for a job in the physiology department, washing dishware and cleaning animal cages. I, who was allergic to the fur of every animal known to man, and who feared all rodents, had to do what I had to do to be where I felt I wanted to get. I shoveled a lot of dog, cat and monkey shit that summer, hated every minute; but my cause was my life, so I was investing, I felt, in my future.

I worked at the Medical School under Professor Clifford Barger, a distinguished research physician-scientist, specialist in microcirculation of the blood. I saw to his animals with a special TLC best I could. Dr. Barger was a warm and wonderful man, and a Jew, rare at that time in that setting. He had gone to the College and the Medical School (HMS) and shared with me stories of quotas that disillusioned me about the democratic institution I had conceived Harvard to be. And yet, he reassured me by his very presence that a Jew could succeed not only at getting into medical school but also at doing research year after year, supported by the National Institutes of Health (NIH), which would lead ultimately to coronation as a full professor.

But the best part of my entrance to the College was in Cambridge in Hollis Hall and in the classroom. There were guys at Hollis from all over New England, the South (Tennessee and Georgia) and the West (California and Washington State), as well as from Europe, especially France and Germany, students of all geographical and ethnic persuasions. Harvard mixed and matched very well. They put me in with Felix from Pennsylvania – a graduate of Exeter, but as socially withdrawn as I was outgoing. We shared our twin-bedded room on the third floor of Hollis, with the names of Ralph W. Emerson and Henry David Thoreau etched a century earlier via a diamond onto the glass panes of our windows.

Felix told me stories, usually late at night, about Exeter and its educational system, very different from that of the Latin School, a system which trained him to write essays with ease, express ideas about politics and philosophy – who was this Kierkegard? - without all the angoisse it was for me with my rigid, rote-oriented classical education at the

Latin School, where we learned to work hard, i.e. memorize, but not to think many original thoughts. The only serious essays I remember writing there were brief book reports in Phil Marsden's English class senior year, in Class I.

So, Felix exemplified another world, stuck pretty much to himself, did brilliantly of course while I struggled with Good and Evil in Western Literature. He would later get the only attic single at Dunster House when we moved out of the Harvard Yard at the end of Freshman Year to the river Houses. He would remain the Dunster hermit for the next three years. He and I had no contact after Freshman Year, none whatever at Harvard or beyond.

He did, I think, envy me my friends, old and new, and my knack for socialization, as I went on to be elected Hollis Hall Entry A representative to the Freshman Union, and Class Secretary thereafter for our Freshman Year. But I struggled with both the humanities and natural sciences, labored hard to do our General Education curriculum justice, and my scholarship was in jeopardy that first year - two B/two C average needed to retain it - unless I could eke out a B minus in our introductory writing class required of all freshmen. I shamelessly pressured my Section Man, a good guy not long since from a tour with the U.S. Navy. I told him of my "situation" and begged him to have mercy and give me a B minus instead of a C plus if I was on the margin which I knew myself to be. I survived with my A's in French Literature saving me from ignominy and went on to do very well after that hard first year.

But all that aside, my brain was humming: I was so excited to be reading the Book of Job, Pilgrim's Progress, the

Divine Comedy, then Camus' The Plague. This was a miracle, to be free to mull the great questions of our day, of any day, really, to read the great minds of human history and to deal with the issue of whether the earth rotated around the sun or vice versa! Our science education at BLS was sadly wanting, so my hook (C) in introductory chemistry for premedical students was an accurate representation of the miserable state of my understanding of chemistry and biology not to mention physics. But, the origin of sin seemed much more important to me in those days than did the mechanisms of chemical bonding – a dichotomy of interests that I maintained well into my later professorship at Columbia.

I continued on with my affection for, and stellar performance in, French, and extended that to Italian, though I failed in my dream of one day being able to read Dante in Italian – failed because between the requirements of my "major" and premedical course requirements, I ran out of flexibility in course selection. Nonetheless, I read Pascal and Voltaire in French, and did a thesis largely in the stacks of Widener Library on Voltaire's literary approaches to his criticisms of the Church.

Many of my happiest, richest moments at Harvard were spent in the stacks at Widener, reading the French masters and just sitting there in my stall, thinking and writing. The world of ideas opened before me, in Widener and in its stacks, and in Harvard classrooms and enchanted me. Pascal and Voltaire were my gods, Camus became one with *La Peste*, I read their books there in French. I was a very excited if embryonic educated man.

I shared this excitement with several good friends

- especially Jack from Akron, a fellow Hollis Haller - who I met regularly for late night, post-Widener closing coffees at Hayes Bickford's across Massachusetts Ave from Widener. Undergraduate life was a period of enthusiasm and mental arousal built around ideas and relationships except when we felt the stress, which was almost constant, of having to do well in midterm exams, papers and final exams, the latter usually making up 40 – 50 percent of our final grades.

I joined the *Cercle francais* of Harvard – drawn to it like a magnet – and was faced with the recognition that I spoke French badly. The Cercle, I came to see, was an enclave of intellectual French-speaking snobs, mostly from private schools in New York, New England and the Continent. With my public school education – American public school not "public school" in the British sense – I was out of my depth linguistically with these guys. On the other hand the Cercle had few members, little money and was virtually moribund. Somehow, in my sophomore year, Andre Gregory, Georges de Montebello and friends – interesting worldly guys whom I liked and who were rabid francophiles - turned to this BLS guy and elected me President du Cercle, an honor that was clearly a mixed bag insofar as the Cercle appeared doomed to even the most casual observer. I, however, took my election seriously and by spring had organized a major event.

The Ballet russe de Montecarlo of Roland Petit was appearing for one week at the Boston Opera House, with Leslie Caron, Lilianne Montevecchi, and the brilliant Colette Marchand, the lover, it was rumored of Roland Petit and a Prima Ballerina of her day. I was intrepid, and armed with my wretched French but my Boston *chutzpah* I went backstage on behalf of the Cercle francais of Harvard, and introduced myself to Roland Petit. I explained in pigeon French that we at Harvard would like to have a reception in honor of the Ballet russe later that week and would he and his dancers be willing to join the Harvard community for a cocktail reception in their honor? By some miracle - I felt - he agreed, and would bring along some of his dancers.

The club members and I went into overdrive and organized the reception at the Goethe Haus on campus. We quickly spread the word by every means then known to man, but especially by plastering posters on trees and buildings around the Yard and in the Houses. Came the appointed evening - around 5 pm as I recall - the wines were poured and the cheeses set out. I escorted Roland Petit and his ensemble to Goethe House from downtown Boston, and voilà! We had a gathering of hundreds! Fellow students, graduate and undergraduate, and faculty, especially from the Department of Romance Languages and Literature. Such enthusiasm and animation, it was glorious. I fell in love with Lilianne - who could resist her? - and between her and Leslie Caron, many a Harvard heart was set aflutter that evening.

And so the Cercle français de Harvard was rejuvenated. One new member of note who was on a fellowship, was a very tall guy, always in a double -breasted suit even in the warmest of days and nights, one Jacques Chirac. He hung out with Andre et al and we welcomed him. He was, however, a very reserved and a quiet guy in those days of his at Harvard.

Later in my career at Harvard and the Cercle I met a charming young Paris-born ingénue who had moved post-War to Brooklyn with her family. They survived the Holocaust by living in Vichy France in the south. The ingenue played a dancer in the Cercle's production of Cocteau's "Le Boeuf sur le Toit." I was enchanted with this Parisian Radcliffe girl and she and I would eventually marry. My spoken French was never up to her standards, however, which should have been a red flag.

Meanwhile on the academic front at Harvard I did passably but not much better than that over the years in the courses needed for medical school: inorganic and organic chemistry, basic biology, and elementary physics, courses in which I felt I was swimming against the current of my brain and heart. Cliff Barger said I could just take the minimum in science and still be able to go to med school – in fact, Harvard encouraged its pre-meds to take a "well-rounded" series of courses, the "get-it-while-you can idea," which was enlightened and a perfect fit for me. I knew I was not a pre-med success – though I did take a Math course and got an A; still, I figured, Harvard was Harvard and from there, wherever.

But my ambivalence showed in another way: as I applied to medical schools my senior year, and ran about dutifully doing interviews, I gave thought to defying Grandma Annie's dictum that I should become a doctor, "we need a doctor in the family", and I applied to both medical school and to graduate school, in literature. I had spent a lot of time in my junior and senior years at Harvard doing an honors thesis on the techniques of literary criticism of Voltaire as he critiqued, largely through satire, the Catholic Church of his day. I wrote my magnum opus in peaceable Widener and there came to love writing. While I got in with ease to graduate lit programs at both Harvard and Columbia, to study for a PhD, the medical school acceptance was elusive until NYU - New York! I was blessed - accepted me, and so I felt at last "the calling."

I am not sure til this day whether it was the medical school admission letter or the fact that the medical school was in New York City that caused me to rejoice. I note, however, that I did have carefully-crafted alternatives: I was accepted at both the Columbia and Harvard Faculties of Arts and Sciences, to do a PhD. in literature. But I elected not to, complying in the end with the family's wishes and, I suppose, with my own deeply programmed commitment to medicine.

If Boston Latin gave me and most of my classmates a sense of well-being, a sense of place in the world, Harvard certainly re-inforced that feeling. The world-as-oyster. But, but, but, but.......There was a price for the lifelong sense of pride in the institution that spawned us and the priceless education it provided. That price was capitulation to the bitch goddess success. True, Harvard did not tell us what career to pursue, it simply and unmistakably said, in a manner of speaking, whatever you do, get back here in 25 or 50 years with a substantial check made out to the Trustees of Harvard College. My classmates and I went a variety of ways: business, law, medicine, science and Government primarily, with fewer – but a notable few - going into academia. I, who had daydreams, as I spent afternoons in chemistry and biology labs, about a career as a writer, saw few poets or painters or musicians in my class.

The figures were these: 82% of us - based on data from our 25th Reunion Class Report, as compiled by Steve Greyser and Tim Ellard - went into Business and Industry (39%), Medicine (16%), Law (13%) and Education (14%), while the remaining 18% would do "other" things - work in Government, be part of the Military, become Clergymen, become CPA's, become politicians. At 25 years out, our median income was more than $60,000 per year, with an average net worth per classmate being $300,000 – in 1981 dollars. And of course the high rollers in the class were busy making gobs of money in stocks and bonds on The Street, with 25% of the Class earning over $100,000 per year, a tidy fortune in those days. However, footnote from a Class survey at the time: 45% of the guys would have opted for a different first job/career if they knew at graduation what they came to know later, at year 25.

Politically, I was born and have remained a serious, lifelong Democrat. During my Harvard years I joined the throngs rooting for Adlai Stevenson - holes in the soles of his shoes added to his charm - as he rode through Harvard Square, though Ike was most everyone else's choice, everyone that is but those in the academic community. Mother advised me to stay away from the political clubs at Harvard, as Uncle Edward Israel had joined something during his years there – I was never sure what that "something" was - that led him to be seen as a Fellow Traveler in certain circles, and she wanted none of that for me.

It was, of course, the era of Joe McCarthy, the scoundrel anti- Communist who defamed many of my professors at the College on no evidence at all. McCarthy had the rabid support of our Catholic brethren in South Boston, who hated the "pinkos" across the Charles, of which I was then one by association. Isabel maintained her equanimity on the subject, and on me, though her father did not. We were all delighted when Joseph Welch of Boston took down Senator McCarthy at the Army-McCarthy hearings in Washington, but it was a bit late for some in our world.

One of the young Section Men Thomas H – you see, I am protecting his identity still! - in my History of Science class was called to testify before the McCarthy Committee when its show rolled into Boston to have at the MIT and Harvard Reds. This Thomas was among the gentlest of human beings and I could not conceive of him as a threat to anyone here or abroad. Still, Roy Cohn hammered him, demanding the names of people who had been in one pinkish club or the other while he and they were undergraduates. Our Section Man resisted all attempts to extract names and was promised a censure by McCarthy and Cohn.

Thomas had missed a class when he had to testify, but was back for the Friday Section Meeting, and the class erupted in applause for him when he walked in, long, sustained applause which brought tears to my eyes – H was suddenly a hero. And ironically no charges were ever filed against him by thc House or Senate as he had done no wrong.

Harvard made me proud that a young Section Man like H could be held in such esteem by the students and faculty, and suffer no punitive measures – that we knew about - from the University in his budding career. I resolved at that moment to disregard my mother's warnings about joining political organizations. I came to feel I had simply to proceed with the peaceful expression of my beliefs. It is the least one can do and retain self-respect, even if under some circumstances there are penalties to endure.

This set the stage for my later involvement in the Civil Rights Movement, when a similar issue arose. I was by then - i.e. after medical school - living in Bethesda, Maryland, and working in the U.S. Public Health Service at the National Institutes of Health, which had rules about its Commissioned Corps Officers not being involved in political activities. The synagogue in Bethesda to which I then belonged had organized a bus to drive those interested into the District for Martin Luther King's March on Washington. It sounds pathetic to have even been minimally concerned about possible violence at the March when civil rights workers, blacks and whites, were being killed in the South, but such was the tenor of the times. Many people, family included, urged me not to go, predicting attacks on marchers and vehicles alike. The March was, in the end, a peaceful, emotionally powerful, statement of support for civil rights and I knew it even as I simply sat under a tree by the Reflecting Pool with hundreds of thousands of blacks and whites, listening in awe to the voice of Martin Luther King, the singing of Peter, Paul and Mary and the poetry of Bob Dylan's *Blowin' in the Wind,* doing what we knew to be right by just being there.

Harvard had inculcated in me or confirmed in me several lines of thinking: First, I was intent on succeeding at a career which was socially prestigious, esteemed even, and if not as financially lucrative as a career in business or finance might have been, one that at least produced a substantial income. Secondly, I wanted to do good works, be physically active and not a relatively passive scholar working in the stacks of a library. Ergo my choice of medicine above the literary life. And, lastly, Harvard, as the Latin School before it, confirmed for me the joy of spending my time with bright and above all interesting people. Thus, the deal was struck and there was not really any turning back.

In retrospect, it was a mixed blessing, because a part of me very much inclined toward the arts and a more Bohemian life. Harvard effectively shut down that inclination for many years to come. Thus, only once I achieved – catch that? – success in my profession – defined by me as becoming a professor at a prestigious university and medical school - would I feel free to give fuller expression to these other passions. I did, however, thoroughly, or almost thoroughly, partake of medical science, while the writerly vein grew in intensity in me as I got older. That was the deal there and I gladly became a physician-scientist, until I no longer could, many years later.

4

Becoming a Physician – Scientist

New York City

My years in the trenches of Anatomy, Physiology, Biochemistry et al were pretty much a horror for me, complemented very occasionally with the triumph of mastering a metabolic pathway, the function of a particular muscle, the mechanism of blood circulation. A language student with little understanding of and passion for science, even from Harvard, was destined at the NYU School of Medicine mostly to suffer during the first two, basic science years. I survived among the sharks of biomedical science - fellow students and superb faculty - by adapting, i.e., by spending more time than I should have at Carnegie Hall concerts, seeing French movies at the Little Carnegie Theater - who could ever forget Martine Carole in "Nana"? - and walking the streets of Greenwich Village looking for a good espresso and a compatible female artist to spend some time with. I just loved New York City. I had a couple of similarly minded pals who ducked out of classes with me. One, Joe T, was an ex-Marine Corps pilot, fresh back from Korea, and Joe and I did a lot together in midtown when we should have been in class on East 30th street. That lasted until second semester when Joe had a schizophrenic break and was hospitalized up in Massachusetts. I did not attribute his "break" to the rigors of medical school but between the Marine Corps Air Force in Korea and the NYU School of Medicine Joe did not have an easy adjustment.

The Associate Dean – an austere gentleman who would precede me at the University of Michigan some years later - called me in late in my first year of Medical School because of my failure in a major Biochemistry exam. He said, in essence, "We accepted you because you did well at Harvard in those studies in which you were interested and we assumed you could transfer that excellence to your medical studies. Time to get on with it."

At that moment I had a decision to make: either devote myself to these courses or take a hike and become a Bohemian. Truth is I was not far from this latter course, but the Bitch Goddess Success was too deeply engrained in my psyche to allow me to walk away. Plus I was beginning to get genuinely interested in the medical sciences, especially physiology and later on pathology. Grandmother's dreams, Boys Latin School, Harvard College and all that jazz had programmed me for professional success so I decided to stick around, even though the science did not come naturally to me, was in fact an interest of recent origin. I figured the rewards for sticking would be in the end what I had bargained for.

Further, and surprisingly to me at the time, within a year

or so the work itself had become interesting to me. At first we simply memorized the pathways of glucose and amino acid metabolism, and the course of spinal nerves and major and minor muscles – for those things the rote methods of Boston Latin School came in handy. We used creative mnemonics such as: "On Old Olympus Towering Top A Fat-Assed German Valsed and Hopped", representing, in their first letters, the "O" for the nerves Olfactory, and Optic, Oculomotor, then Trochlear, Trigeminal, Abducens, Facial, Auditory (Vestibulocochlear), Glossopharyngeal, Vagus, Accessory, and Hypoglossal. Even to this day one remembers! We were becoming focused increasingly on pathophysiology and how diseases came about. The changes that occurred in nerves and muscles when afflicted with arthritis, neurodegenerative disorders like Lou Gehrig's disease, the hormonal disorders like diabetes, the pathology of such catastrophes were somehow exciting to study – not just as abstractions but as we were to see them in real patients on the wards at Bellevue. I could feel myself gaining in enthusiasm for the study of these things, and I finally felt good being there in medical school. Unlike the character in the Alec Guinness movie, Men in White, in which Alec received an annual stipend every year he remained in medical school, I was surely not motivated by economic considerations or prospects which were far from my Bohemian thought processes both at Harvard and at NYU.

I thus gave myself finally over to the work of becoming a physician. For me it was very hard. I had been doing just enough barely to get by; but what I had to do now was to sweat, because enzyme kinetics, acid-base balance, myocardial muscle physiology - those things were anathema to me. My sense was they did come easily to the majority of my classmates, at least that was how it seemed. Most of my medical school classmates had had tunnel vision for years: they were intent from about age twelve on becoming physicians. I, however, was a serious waffler, propelled by family and outside pressures but by no means having a single-track mind in the matter. If anything I would rather have done other.

To make matters worse for me there was a certain insouciance practiced by my peers. They seemed to do little hard work yet easily passed if not excelled in these studies, mostly with superb grades. The extreme was in the NYU Residence Hall where many classmates hung out. A poker game was ongoing there, 24/7, and while I did not play - of course! - I admired the late night games, the cigar smoking, and beer drinking. These were the kinds of medical students I longed to be but which I could not be - for me to pass, just to pass, I would have to labor hard and focus, it had become clear to me.

Worth noting that I was to be married to my ingénue at the end of year 01 and I was determined to play a bit before then. Still, Dean Hubbard made clear that he and I needed resolution by final exams - the future, my future, in medicine was in the balance.

While it is true that I floundered much of that first year, part of the problem was situational. I had arrived in New York with no place to live - like most everyone who arrives there friendless and unknown - and so the Housing Office, i.e. the Bulletin Board at the School, referred me to one Mrs. Margaret Gratton over on First Avenue in nearby Stuyvesant Town. Mrs. G had a room to sublet, her pastor husband having died six months earlier of cancer, and so she had his former study to rent out to an unsuspecting student. The arrangement was I would pay $12.50 a week for the room, and an added fee for any meals I took with her. She made, she told me at the initial interview, the world's best blueberry pie, a favorite of mine of long-standing. So I moved in, ate a rare meal but a frequent blueberry pie, and tried to mind my own business, study some evenings, go out and about town on others.

But that was not to be allowed. Mrs. Gratton wanted not a tenant but a surrogate son/husband, someone with whom to discuss her life and the state of her world. And she wanted a lot of praise for her blueberry pie. I would sometimes be studying my anatomy books and the call would come from the kitchen, "Arthur, how about a nice piece of blueberry pie, specially made this afternoon for you!" This was said in a plaintive voice, one not to be dismissed lightly. So, blueberry pie it was, along with a nice scoop of vanilla ice cream. With one or two such slices and scoops my fragile will was broken and I could not realistically return to enzyme kinetics.

I had to get out of there, and quickly or my first year –and I - would go down the tube. A friend from Harvard knew of a family – two doctors with two college age kids - that had a brownstone on the Upper East Side. The two kids were off at college, so the doctors wanted someone to occupy a room on the fourth floor so as to have a presence in the brownstone most of the time. As a medical student I seemed to fit their bill perfectly. Little did they know I was a gadabout, intent on discovering the City, and not a nerd who would sit there and study all the time. For impoverished me though, at $5 a week, it was a steal, so I headed with my stuff uptown to my room on East 64th Street, between Park and Lexington no less, for the balance of the academic year.

Having somehow managed that first year to pass Biochemistry, and all the rest; and having gotten married in the Orthodox style, I moved into second year more committed than I had ever been to my métier. The farther into second year we got the more patient contact we had. That helped me a very lot. By the time the third year came upon us we were ready for two or three month rotations in Surgery, Internal Medicine, Obstetrics and Gynecology, and especially, for me, Pediatrics.

Surprising to me the taking care of children on the wards and in the nurseries at Bellevue was a joy. To be of use to the children and babies was a privilege I never expected to have, because the younger ones spoke little and the practice of pediatrics was a bit like veterinary medicine: one often had to make diagnoses without benefit of statements from the patients. On the other hand, these kids usually had one thing wrong not a list of geriatric complaints, and once one dealt with the primary issue - sometimes complex cardiac disease, rare tumors, sudden onset infectious diseases - the kids could usually go home and live their lives. It was also true that I performed much better at the bedside in clinical medicine than I had in the basic science curriculum, so my grades went shooting upwards and I became a highly competent third, then fourth year medical student.

In the course of this panoply of training I found myself becoming interested in the origins, especially the genetic origins, of many diseases we saw. We had had some lectures earlier on in the emerging field of RNA (and DNA) analysis and of genetic control of protein synthesis, since we had a to-be-Nobel Prize Laureate on the NYU Faculty, Severo Ochoa, a much - traveled exile from Spain, of distinguished pedigree, who was a major figure in the new field of biochemical genetics. His talks were spellbinding. I found myself unexpectedly excited, on the one hand, by the emerging understanding of the most important molecules of human life and reproduction, and, on the other, by the potential it gave us to explain mechanisms of genetic disease, especially in pediatric patients.

Late in my junior year I did an elective in pediatric research related to a metabolic disease that killed those afflicted at an early age. Professor (of Pediatrics) Joseph Dancis had devoted his lab to sorting out the nature of this heretofore unknown disorder called Maple Syrup Urine Disease (MSUD), in which infants, born normally, rapidly developed seizures and severe neurologic damage that precluded their growth and development and ended invariably in early death. Dancis identified several amino, and their derived keto, acids as being the culprits in this rare disorder: leucine, isoleucine and valine. There were enzymes responsible for breakdown of these amino acids – well, one particular enzyme involved with the metabolism of all three of these amino acids - and he reasonably hypothesized that the inability to metabolize these amino acids, which likely became toxic at high concentrations, was due to that enzyme deficiency – as several other disorders of amino acid metabolism were then being shown to be caused by.

Dancis wanted me to work on identification of the carriers for this recessively inherited disorder, i.e., both parents had to be carriers for the child to be affected, and together they would have a 25 percent risk of having an affected infant with each pregnancy but only if each of the abnormal genes was contributed by each parent. Dancis helped me learn new lab techniques to measure these amino acids and their derivative keto acids, and had me study a Maple Syrup Disease family from southern New Jersey whose little girl was on a restricted amino acid diet under his care at Bellevue.

I worked for months in my "spare time" perfecting a method to measure the involved amino acids in blood and urine. Our assumption/hypothesis was that those who carried a single copy of the (abnormal) gene for MSUD would have an intermediate level of the enzyme and thus an intermediate degree of amino acid elevation in blood and urine. We might be able, if he were correct, to be able to identify carriers and determine their degree of risk of having an affected baby – so we could counsel them accordingly.

I conducted my first studies on the New Jersey family at Bellevue, giving the parents a loading dose of oral leucine, isoleucine and valine and then measuring their levels in blood and urine at various times after the ingestion of the load. I expected that their rate of breaking down the administered load would be halfway between that of an affected child and a perfectly normal individual. I followed up by going to Philadelphia Children's Hospital where I repeated this work on a slightly expanded version of their family. That was my first trip to do genetical research and it was the beginning of a heady time for me.

Now, the family had originated in Eastern North Carolina, and to do a complete family profile using the loading test approach I would have to travel to North Carolina and do these studies on the bulk of relatives there, including grand-parents, aunts and uncles. The mother and father of the New Jersey baby both came originally from the same town in Eastern Carolina - the number of possible carriers there exceeded twenty, given all the sibs of these parents.

One spring day in my senior year at medical school I loaded up my little Vauxhall sedan with boxes of lab equipment, including carefully measured doses of leucine, isoleucine and valine, as well as of methionine also suspected of being involved in MSUD, and I trundled off toward Plymouth, NC, where I would find the subjects to be studied. I was very excited because not only was this my first major expedition as a budding human geneticist, it was also my first time in America's Deep South. And the family to be studied was a black family, which added to my uncertainty about the upcoming experience: A black family in rural North Carolina might, even with the full and enthusiastic endorsement of the New Jersey branch of the family, be a challenge in the then white world of Southern Medicine. Would the family cooperate with a young white doctor from New York? Where would we be able to work? Lots of questions before departure.

The drive down was nonetheless calm until I arrived at the Hampton Ferry to cross Chesapeake Bay to Norfolk.

On that ferry, I saw the bathrooms marked "White" and "Colored", as well as the water fountains, similarly marked. I vaguely knew of this stuff but had had no first-hand experience of it. I became agitated but continued on my way, arriving some hours later in the Town of Plymouth, where I went to the local hospital, Washington County Hospital - also segregated - to meet the doctor who would lead me to my residence and to my workspace for the week.

He said the medical staff, whose guest I was, had decided to put me up at the Plymouth Country Club, which sounded splendid. The Club was, as many were, a golf club with a very few rooms for guests. I settled in and agreed to meet the president of the medical staff the next day at breakfast at the Club to work out arrangements whereby I could do the amino acid load testing on the local family in the confines of the Washington County Hospital Emergency Room.

As I was to learn, the Town of Plymouth - population then about 2500 - was 65 percent black, 30 percent white, but you would never have known that. The Country Club was staffed by black waiters and the one other guest was white, while, as it turned out, the Washington County Hospital where I was to do my work was completely off limits to blacks: there were no black patients, no black doctors or nurses. That was carefully explained to me by the Chief of Staff at our breakfast the next morning. But, he arranged for the J Family to enter the Emergency Room area for their studies, so long as they were separate at all times from the patients.

Now, Washington County Hospital was not a large county hospital, having only 25 beds, so the ER was not exactly filled to capacity. Nonetheless, I was assigned a workspace there for my lab supplies, a satisfactory centrifuge to concentrate my serum and urinary specimens, and a place to draw blood and obtain urine specimens from the Family. Meanwhile, I asked a lot of questions of the Family to fill in the details of the pedigree, and I answered a lot of questions about what these tests might show, how the baby girl was doing in New York, etc. A full first day, with five subjects participating, at hourly intervals.

One of the key persons on the pedigree was an elderly gentleman, Grandpa Rufus, who was in his 90's, lived not far away but I would have to go to him as he moved about with the greatest of difficulty. I set an appointment with him for that evening via his daughter who was one of the five of the first day, and I went off to see him. He was a slender man of medium height, with a much-lined face, snow-white hair, a thin white moustache, and a gentle, peaceable way about him. He greeted me warmly and offered me a rocker by his side on the front porch of the cabin he shared with Gramma Lucia.

Rufus told me how pleased he was to have "the young doctor from New York" come down to Plymouth to help his family. He asked what these studies were all about and I explained the rationale to him. He appreciated the help for the baby in New York and the help for his offspring here in the Carolinas.

I asked Rufus about his origins, whether he had been born in North Carolina. He told me, No, he had been born in Georgia, at a very difficult time for the black man. He told me how it was for him as a slave picking cotton in the hot fields of Georgia, and how, at the age of 24, he and Lucy had one day simply slipped away and migrated "north" via the Underground Railroad, a series of homesteads on route where a black man and his family could hide from those tracking him. Unlike many of his friends, he decided to stop running once he got away from the worst of it, and so he settled in Eastern Carolina – he had no stomach for the industrial north - where the weather was good, the sea was nearby, there were not many people, and he could build his own cabin on a small piece of land he would sublet and live in peace with his wife and, later, eight children. He then went inside his cabin and brought out a musket to show me. He told me he used to shoot animals with that musket, especially squirrels and gophers, to feed the family. He also explained, with a wink, how it was his weapon to defend his crew against intruders, if I knew what he meant, and I surely did.

Sitting on the porch of Grandpa Rufus' cabin, sipping an iced tea as the sun set in the distance, I could not help but think about something I had come to see in New York City, namely, that so much of life depended on chance: the happenstance of who one's parents were, the seemingly random nature of where and to whom a man or woman was born. I had had patients in New York, mainly youngish men, who lived in a world of heroin addiction and alcoholism – and while I might have been tempted at one time to judge them, even occasional visits to their rat- and roach-infested apartments made me realize that they or any of us would likely find it impossible to emerge from these places and still live the kind of life anyone would regard as reasonable. I often said to myself in the face of such degradation that had I been born to such families in such places I undoubtedly would have become what these young men had become: alcoholics with cirrhosis by age 25 or addicts with withdrawal symptoms whenever the money ran out.

Now, here in Plymouth, North Carolina, another pathway showed its head. Rufus was a free man, infinitely better off than a desperately poor black man in New York City; but he could not eat at the local restaurant in his town, and could not get help medically at the local hospital - accidents of birth? Maybe, maybe not. Still, to be born into a black family in Eastern North Carolina as his children were was an infinitely better deal than to start life in the tenements of the big cities of the Northeast and Midwest. Neither was a bargain but I now had more appreciation for Rufus's son Rudy - father of the affected baby in New Jersey, someone I had come to know in the course of our caring for his daughter at Bellevue - Rudy who in turn left North Carolina for southern New Jersey, where he worked in accounting and struggled to pay at least something for the care of his MSUD daughter Maya.

I wondered, on the cabin porch that evening and in the next few that I shared with Rufus, what my own children when I had them would turn out to be. They would have the benefits, economic and intellectual, of smart, educated parents, even accomplished parents in all likelihood; but while those things guaranteed nothing they at least would give my sons and daughters a start in life that was alien to the children of Rufus and Lucia and even unto their grandchildren.

One thing that must have made a huge difference to

Rufus's family was the presence of books in the house. When I went inside for a moment I saw a shelf with the Holy Bible, several hymnals, a book on Eli Whitney and the cotton gin, and one or two other books. Rufus told me that he read the Bible to his children every night before bedtime, and that they all prayed together on Sundays at the local African Methodist (AME) Church over in nearby Edenton. The children learned to read and write and these were values that Rufus and Lucy proudly conveyed daily.

I felt a certain warmth as well as respect for this man and his family, and as I completed my studies in Plymouth, I grew closer to them, especially to Rufus himself, and I promised him I would do everything possible to help his grandbaby in New Jersey, would share our findings about carrier identification with the rest of the family. The man from Georgia, with the musket, made a deep impression on the young not-yet-doctor from Boston.

During the next last days in Plymouth I ate grits for breakfast – hated them – and barbecued ribs in the evenings, often with Rufus at his cabin. I worked on the specimens obtained from 18 of the 20 potential subjects - two declined to participate; and in general I was treated like a visiting dignitary by the medical people at Washington County Hospital and I was grateful.

So, during an unlikely week in the Deep South, my career as an itinerant human geneticist was launched.

I thus had gone in those few years from a struggling first year medical student to a candidate for the Senior Research Prize – I did not get it but to come in a very close second, with the support of Professor Ochoa who read and supported my research paper on the genetics of MSUD was of great inspiration to me. I finished medical school with much more confidence in my scientific ability than I had had when I entered. I was ready to do medicine and science in tandem.

• • •

During these years at Harvard College and then at the New York University School of Medicine, I was supported by numerous scholarships. Both Harvard and NYU were generous and I remain grateful to them for easing my financial burdens during those formative years. While I was in medical school the financial support of the Leopold Schepp Foundation of New York, a private foundation, helped me survive.

5

Being a Physician – Scientist

Baltimore – Bethesda

My internship year in pediatrics at Bellevue in New York was an education, in many ways. First, I saw so many sick kids both in the out-patient clinics and on the Bellevue wards that I learned to manage complex childhood diseases as well as routine clinical problems with facility. Second, I learned to function on not much sleep, sometimes not knowing the next day what medications I had called in during the night to treat a problem case. The 80 - 100 hour work week for interns was then standard, but the House Staff at New York City Hospitals was organizing, hiring legal representation to both cut our hours and raise our pay from $1800 per annum. Over the years that followed the Intern and Residents' Committee - our labor union, really - would gain momentum, with a steadily rising salary for house staff and a cap on the number of working hours allowed. But, by the time these changes took effect, I was long gone, down to Baltimore,

Bethesda and other sites on the Mason Dixon Line and beyond.

My departure from New York was in the normal course of my medical training. In the fall of internship year at Bellevue, I had to decide if I would stay there for residency or go elsewhere. Truth was that while I learned an enormous amount by tending to the sick children at Bellevue, I had no time to read about the diseases I was seeing and the teaching was less formal, we learned mostly by experience. I decided to look around at other residency programs, places I might have more bedside teaching and have a few moments each day to do at least a little reading. I applied to Hopkins and the Boston Children's Hospital.

The reputation of Hopkins as a training center in pediatrics was formidable, especially in genetics to which I was now drawn. When I arrived in Baltimore for the interviews, Professor Barton Childs, the guru of pediatric genetics then and later, handed me a piece of chalk, pointed to his office blackboard, and said, explain to me what you have found in your Maple Syrup Disease studies, with Joe Dancis. I was intimidated but this was my own work and I could talk for hours about it - except now I had an audience of one who knew a lot more than I did about inherited metabolic diseases. It was intimidating but exciting - then and always - to share with a man such as Childs my work on carrier detection.

There was a feeling there at Hopkins, I could detect it even during my interview day, a certain pride of institution, not unlike that feeling of institutional pride I had had at BLS and Harvard, less at NYU. That feeling focused both on its present and in no small measure on its past. Hopkins was, after all, a world created by many giants of modern medicine: Sir William Osler, the internist; William Halstead, the surgeon; Harvey Cushing, the neurosurgeon; Alfred Blalock, the cardiac surgeon; and William Welch, the pathologist. These men, in concert with the imposing statue of Jesus that greeted the visitor to the Hospital at its entrance – I could never quite get used to that one, I confess – gave the Johns Hopkins Hospital an aura that existed at no other hospital I had ever been at, to then or since, for that matter.

But above all it was Barton's interest in my work and the genuine enthusiasm for its young doctors that the Hopkins faculty communicated via its teaching and hands on approach to training and patient care that distinguished Hopkins from other medical institutions I knew or had heard about. So, when, two weeks after my interview, I received a telegram from Robert Cooke, chief of pediatrics, inviting me to join the House Staff the following July, well, there was little doubt I would accept. And so, I trundled off to Baltimore the following summer, delighted at the prospect.

Note: the arrogance of the Boston Children's staff during my interview there was unpleasant, even for this Bostonian, so however much I respected that institution, I felt disinclined to return to Boston to surround myself with their pomposity for my Residency years. It was the "sumus primi" thing rearing its head again, and, well, I suppose I had had enough of that already.

World events were to make my initial stay at Hopkins a brief one. The Berlin crisis was developing and the need for doctors in the military was growing, resulting in the doctor draft. I applied for a commission in the U.S. Public Health

Service in October, requesting a deferment until completion of my residency at Hopkins two years later. However, the U.S. Army also sent me a telegram ordering me to report on Monday, December 18, 1961, at 9:00 a.m. to First Army Headquarters on Staten Island for induction.

Those words "for induction" sent a shiver through my body when I read the telegram, and they still do to this day. However, having already completed my application to the Commissioned Corps of the Public Health Service (PHS), I was able to prod the Service to activate my commission by December 18th, with the knowledge that if I were on active duty in the PHS the Army could not insist on my induction. The PHS was acceptable to the feds as a uniformed quasi-military organization. Commissioned Corps Officers had appointments equivalent to U.S. Naval rankings - I would go in as Lieutenant Commander (!), at the Surgeon level - and depending where I was assigned could or would have to wear the uniform of a U.S. Naval Officer. So the PHS was a hedge against a full-scale military activation and one which would allow me to continue to develop my research career.

I had, however, to be on active duty and thus had to leave residency at Hopkins, my new-found "home". For a young man who had stuck to the straight and narrow path - high school to college to medical school to internship to residency, with no time off for good behavior - cutting the cord and heading for a time of uncertainty was nerve-shattering. Plus, when I did appear at the PHS Headquarters in Washington they had no idea whatsoever what to do with me. Since I had expressed an interest in genetics, they were open to my exploring the relatively new field of radiation genetics as applied to humans. The Division of Radiological Health was my official sponsor and I began to explore the research options in radiation genetics, especially the then emerging field of radiation human genetics.

I discussed my situation with Barton and he suggested a graduate course in modern genetics that spring at the Homewood Campus of Hopkins, plus he urged me to visit, at the National Institutes of Health (the NIH) in Bethesda, the cytogeneticist Joe Hin Tjio - a Chinese agronomist from Java who had recently (1956) discovered that we humans normally have 46 chromosomes - not 48, as had been the number accepted for many years. This was a discovery he made while working at the University of Lund in Sweden, in the laboratory of Albert Levan. Tjio grew fetal lung cells to make their chromosomes apparent, and it was a discovery which opened the field of human cytogenetics to a wide range of studies, particularly in children with birth defects and in patients with cancer. In my instance, given the background years of radiation genetic experiments on fruit flies and mice, Tjio's methods for growing human cells allowed the scientific world to examine directly human cells exposed to radiations of various origins. <u>Note:</u> *In order to visualize the chromosomes of human cells the nuclei of cells must be put into division because during cell division the chromosomes separate and then may be readily visualized, counted, analyzed, etc. Stimulating the largely non-dividing cells of the body to divide in tissue culture enabled the detailed analysis of the chromosomes.*

I received US PHS permission to take the Hopkins genetics course, but went on my own to see Tjio to discuss the possibility of my working with him. When I called his lab to set up the appointment, he was less than enthusiastic about even the interview itself. He was reclusive, as I had been warned, not much wanting contact. But Tjio knew and respected the work of Barton Childs at Hopkins and so that opened his door the necessary crack for me to get in and at least talk with him.

It was awkward with him from the beginning. To his credit he knew I knew nothing in genetics; and when he asked what I would like to work on while with him, if we could agree on a project, I proposed, vaguely, something related to radiation exposure and cytogenetics. I explained further that I was already in a salaried position with the PHS and would come at no expense to him or his budget, except for lab supplies and a microscope. Tjio asked in detail about my background, but was more interested in sharing his with me - a one-sided sharing which would go on throughout most of my two-year stay in his lab at NIH. I learned in detail about the pain of his own miserable two years under the Japanese occupation of Indonesia.

Tjio described for me the lives of his Chinese-born parents and his own birth in Indonesia; his studies at Bogor College on plant breeding and agronomy; and the details of his imprisonment and torture during the Japanese occupation of Java. Having somehow survived those war years in his native but occupied Dutch East Indies, he had gone upon liberation on a Red Cross refugee ship from Indonesia to Holland. From Holland, he quickly moved to Zaragoza, Spain, working for ten years in plant genetics/cytogenetics, prior to his eventual move to Sweden, to pursue cell culture work with Levan.

I felt humbled in the face of such a life story. My story until then was much more pedestrian. But, as time went on, I came to see that Hin, as he preferred to be called, was not unmarked from his experiences and his travels: he was a very difficult man to get along with.

Over the next years, often while we worked late in the lab, he told me more. He had gotten into a fearful fight with Levan who had been absent for some months while Tjio did the lab work in Sweden on the dividing human cells. His co-workers at Lund had urged Tjio to quickly publish his results on the fetal cell chromosome number lest he be scooped by others working on the problem. However, Levan insisted that he Levan be senior author on the ground-breaking paper, it being his lab. And that was often the custom in European laboratories where the professor reigned supreme. Tjio was having none of it, however, and felt that since he had done the research he should be lead author, which he eventually was.

The publication of his results pushed Tjio into the forefront of the new field of human cytogenetics, and many urged him to emigrate to the States. He told me, however, that he knew a lot about the Red Scare created by Senator McCarthy of Wisconsin and he had no wish to go to a country where such hysterical anti-Communism prevailed. Hermann Muller of the University of Indiana, a distinguished (fruit fly) geneticist known the world over, urged Hin to reconsider, and when Ted Puck of the University of Colorado invited him to continue his work in cell culture and cytogenetics at Colorado, Hin finally accepted, enrolling at the University also to get his PhD. While in Scandinavia Tjio had married an Icelandic woman named Inga – a wonderful woman, a biologist, who smoked little cigarillos - and they had a slow-to-develop son named YuHin, so Tjio felt that being in the U.S. would be better for himself and the family.

Early in the 1960's Hin was invited to join the National Institute of Arthritis and Metabolic Diseases at N.I.H. in Bethesda, and his modest lab soon became one of a very few existing centers for research on human chromosomes. By the time I came on the NIH scene Tjio , Inga, and YuHin were established in an apartment on the NIH campus, in Building 30, where they were to live for many years until Hin's retirement in the early 1990's.

I am not sure how Hin saw me initially but he accepted me provisionally as a Guest Worker, and insisted that before I could start working in his lab I had to complete the genetics course at Hopkins AND write an acceptable research proposal – acceptable not to my PHS superiors who, he felt, would know no genetics but a project acceptable to him. So I spent the next months that winter and spring of 1962 commuting up to Hopkins for the course, and doing literature searches on radiation genetics at the National Library of Medicine (LOM), on the campus of NIH. The outline of a radiation effects proposal began to percolate in my mind and eventually, later that spring, with guidance from both Childs and Tjio I embarked.

The central question was whether we were likely to see in human cells the same kinds of chromosomal abnormalities inducible in the cells of fruit flies (*Drosophila),* yeast (*Tradescantia*), and irradiated mice. I had reviewed the world's literature on the effects of radiations on genetic systems and knew that mutations of the chromosomes might be significant if produced in human cells - with their biological and clinical significance yet to be determined. The assumption was that induced mutations were not useful and probably even deleterious. I proposed that my work would be done on the blood cells of NIH patients exposed to diagnostic levels of x-ray. As this work would lead to my first scientific paper it was of special significance to me. Preliminary work in humans exposed to higher levels of radiations suggested we might well see such chromosome damage even at lower dose levels.

I was delighted to be working at last in a proper lab, in a proper institution. My period of study and thinking was mercifully past and I could get my hands dirty again, as I had done at NYU on Maple Syrup Disease. (That study ended up being published by Dancis under his own name and I did not even get a co-authorship, though I had done virtually all of the work.) But now I had grown weary of reading at the LOM and of thinking without doing. It was the old Widener v Medicine issue for me. Now I would be able to handle specimens, analyze samples objectively, and draw my own conclusions about the presence or absence of effects. My "handlers" at the Division of Radiological Health were delighted and Tjio was supportive, and demanding as well in terms of the quality of my slides and chromosome preparations. He was a stickler for quality in these samples, a thrust which I came to feel was totally necessary if the results of the research were to be reproducible.

The next year and a half with Tjio were complex: on the one hand he welcomed me into his lab and personal family and introduced me to his occasional visitors, people often of distinction. I particularly enjoyed meeting Professor Donald Keene of Columbia, the translator par excellence of many Japanese novels of the day and Noh plays of the past, who could do analyses of Japanese literature in English or Japanese at both of which he was proficient. Keene wrote about Japanese literature broadly as well as in specific, with translations of the plays of Chikamatsu, Noh plays which came to interest me during my stay in Hiroshima. Keene was also a translator of the novels of Kawabata and Abe. I would more fully appreciate Keene's work when, some few years later, I was to go to Japan to live and work in Hiroshima and would become a regular at the wonderful Maruzen Bookstore on the Hondori pedestrian mall in the center of town.

As I think back to the time with Tjio I have to say it was a blessing to be with so sophisticated a scientist and Renaissance-type scholar of many interests not only in science but also in literature and the arts. And yet there was something askew in him. There were only three of us in the lab: his technician Joey Mason from D.C., a black man who had a degree from the University of Maryland; Jacqueline Whang-Peng, a Chinese from Taiwan - a cancer cytogeneticist who was warm and welcoming and a kind of intermediary between Tjio and the NIH world. To them he was somewhat reluctantly adding me, the white Jewish medical doctor from Hopkins. I would have to convince him I would be worth his efforts at mentoring.

My work went along well: I had a corner of the lab in which to sit hovered over the microscope, analyzing the chromosomes of x-rayed patients at the NIH Clinical Center. I worked out the arrangements to draw blood samples from patients after chest x-rays, fluoroscopy exams, renal studies, etc. More than that, it turned out I was finding chromosomal abnormalities in samples – I was reading them blindly, without reference to the exposure status of the patients at the time of blood drawings and it amazed me and Hin that even at diagnostic levels of x-rays the human chromosome was susceptible to damage.

For the better part of my first year, Hin and I got along decently. I was invited over occasionally to have a lunch with the Tjios, even a drink in the evenings from time to time. Then my first child, a daughter, was born across the street at the National Naval Medical Center and Tjio took some marvelous black and white photographs of her, photos the family would always cherish. But indirectly her birth led to an almost permanent break between Hin and myself.

Turned out that my daughter had large bluish discolorations over her buttocks, marks called Mongolian spots, spots that would disappear during childhood. These spots are seen in Asian peoples – 90 percent of Asian infants have these spots - at a much higher rate than among Caucasians, 5-10 percent. And 95 percent of black babies have these spots. Tjio insisted that the presence of these Mongolian spots indicated that there were genes of Oriental origin running in my family. I said I knew of no such origins in my family but all was possible in peoples of Eastern European origin, so why not?

That acknowledgement was not enough for him and he felt I was being anti-Asian by not fully embracing his suggestion. It did not matter at all to me whence came those spots but Hin felt slighted and completely stopped talking to me. There followed one of the most painful periods I have endured, having to be around someone who has unilaterally closed the door on our relationship. No matter what I said to Hin he would not soften his stance and resume our relationship. We worked in close quarters so this was awful, but I resolved to complete my work in the six months I had remaining and we would see beyond that what would be. In the end, we had to communicate about the results of my/our study and we did, sufficiently to allow me to submit the manuscript to the New England Journal of Medicine, which accepted it forthwith.

I have often thought over the years about Tjio's revelations regarding his time in Japanese prisons in Java. Like most Westerners my familiarity in such matters had largely been confined to German prison camps and the Holocaust - but here was the Asian version before my eyes, with the personal memories of a distinguished man of science, a man of intellect and culture, a man I respected greatly. And so, when the Public Health Service would later suggest that I actually go to Japan to apply what I had learned in Tjio's lab, I was very hesitant if not scared, anxious at what kind of people I would find there, how we would get on. We Americans had, after all, bombed the Japanese into surrender, after which we occupied their country.

But first, as my time at NIH wound down I was approached by my seniors at the Division of Radiological Health who asked if I might be interested in a longer career in the Public

Health Service: The Commissioned Corps would pay me a salary while I completed my residency at Hopkins and I would, in turn, owe the Service two years upon completion of the residency. By this time in my personal life I had one child and a second on the way and so the idea of remaining on active duty but salaried as a Senior Surgeon in the PHS was not at all unattractive. After due consideration - took about a minute - I agreed and my orders were "cut", assigning me back to Hopkins as of January 1.

I intended, best I could foretell, to continue my career in genetics. Molecular genetics was increasingly the rage at that time so I approached Dr Chris Anfinsen at NIH, who would go on in 1972 to be awarded a Nobel Prize in chemistry, asking if I could join his lab on my return to NIH two years later, i.e. 1965. When he agreed I was delighted to have booked a place with another distinguished scientist.

My residency at Hopkins would come first. An endlessly fascinating period of learning pediatrics and practicing it. As it was coming to a close a bit later I began to feel that I somehow could not go back to Bethesda and the suburban world there, the world of Giant Food and all that jazz. It was an impossibility for me. I had become a serious doc while at Hopkins, and wanted somehow to combine medicine and genetics with some clinical activity, maybe on a Public Health Service Indian Reservation in the Southwest, I did not know. But I had been lucky enough to secure a place in Anfinsen's lab, and that was a sacrosanct commitment for a lucky young scientist.

But, during a winter visit to Rad Health one of the people who had helped me early on in activation of my commission asked if I would be interested in going to Japan where the cytogenetic studies of the A-bomb survivors was languishing for want of someone trained to do such studies. Initially, I was really put off by the suggestion: I had grown up in Boston at a time when the Japanese were our sworn enemies, people who had committed atrocities of incredible horror on prisoners like Tjio and our own soldiers at Corregidor and Bataan and across Asia. But as the weeks went by and I discussed Japan with people who knew it, and began reading about its history and literature, I began to wonder if going over there, and setting up my own labs in Hiroshima and Nagasaki, would not be a very exciting thing to do – far from Giant Foods and suburban Maryland to be sure, about as far as one could get, and doing work which the scientific world was waiting on. Finally, I agreed to go for a term of two years.

That left me the unpleasant job of telling Anfinsen that I would not, in fact, be joining his lab – turning down a plum position like that was no easy matter, and telling him was very unpleasant in that he turned his back on me and walked out of the room. But, I had become convinced that I wanted to see a bit of the world while doing my professional work. I had found a Japanese teacher for my wife and me from the School of Public Health at Hopkins, and while Kenji taught us Japanese he also told us stories about the War on Shikoku where he was from, as it affected him and his father who was pilot of a Mitsubishi fighter plane.

The momentum grew. My wife and then two daughters and I geared up to take leave of the world as we knew it; and when the orders came through from Washington, we had bookings on Pan Am via Hawaii to Tokyo, thence to Hiroshima.

Haiku

In the cicada's cry
There's no sign that can foretell
How soon it must die.

BASHO, 17th century

6

A U.S. Public Health Servant in Japan

Hiroshima, Mon Amour

I spent much of my youth in Boston hating the Germans and the Japanese. The Germans were an obvious target for this Jewish *cheder* boy who lost no family that he knew about in the Holocaust, but imagined that he did, back in Poland and Russia. The Japanese, however, were hated for their sneak attack on Pearl Harbor and for their reported cruelty on the death marches of Corregidor and Bataan.

On December 7th, 1941, I sat with my parents at the radio in the Epstein's apartment next door to ours on Morton Street in Dorchester, as we huddled together with Louis and Polly Epstein and their beautiful daughter Frances listening to President Roosevelt describe the disaster that had been perpetrated by the Japanese. In the next few years we were to learn on the nightly news of the bayonetting of babies in China and throughout Southeast Asia; we learned, too, of the incredible death tolls of American and English soldiers in the Philippines and Solomon Islands and throughout the

South Pacific. No, a young man playing "War" on the streets of Boston had no choice but to hate the bastards. And then, somehow, twenty years later, I found myself on the streets of Hiroshima, the Hiroshima which had been utterly destroyed by the first atomic bomb ever dropped on a civilian population. More than 100,000 were killed immediately. I was there, with others, to see what the longer term effects were, in my case the genetic effects. And yet the human story was too powerful to neglect. This was not simply a study of the effects of radiation exposure in a large human population: Hiroshima was a city struggling in 1965 to find its place again among the great cities of Japan.

It was self-evident that the city would be newly built, for the most part - there were sections in the near suburbs that had been left intact but nil downtown - and yet I felt no animosity as I went to work each day at the then Atomic Bomb Casualty Commission (ABCC) on Hijiyama Hill overlooking the city. My children felt the animosity of their Japanese classmates at *Yochien*, the nursery school they attended, but that was the stuff of being a foreigner in the relatively closed world of Japanese homogeneity. As I dealt daily with other scientists at the Commission - an agency funded by the U.S. National Academy of Sciences and run by the U.S. Atomic Energy Commission and the Japanese National Institutes of Health - I felt perfectly comfortable, encouraged really, not at all threatened, and so I was able to settle into a routine, creating my cytogenetics laboratory, with a small but important staff whom I could train as I wished.

The key person in the lab - and a very important person in

my personal life in Japan – was one Shozo Iida. Iida-san was assigned to be my head technician by Howard Hamilton the Chief of Clinical Laboratories and my on-site boss in Hiroshima and Nagasaki. Iida-san was a long-time technician at ABCC, having arrived back in Japan after his time as a Japanese Army chef in Manchuria, where he served. Iida-san's father was originally part of the Japanese occupation force in Manchuria and Iida-san grew up in China, becoming a Japanese Army man as the war wore on and he came of age. Somehow Iida-san's English was very good, and we could speak freely with one another. He went to great lengths to tend to my family and to have his family interact with my own.

We set to work right away putting in place the procedures for growing blood cells in tissue culture, for harvesting those cells and examining their chromosomes under the microscope. It was a modification of the methods I had implemented in Tjio's laboratory in Bethesda, but on a much grander scale. Fortunately, Iida-san was an excellent black and white photographer and we could take beautiful pictures of the chromosomes to show our prowess to the world at ABCC, and later well beyond.

On my first August 6th in Hiroshima – the 20th anniversary of the dropping of the A-bomb – I wandered with Iida-san, downtown to the Peace Park where the annual ceremony was to be held. While I had visited earlier one weekend in late July, seen the various monuments, I was there at 08:00 on the sixth on a different kind of mission: to feel the force of the A-bomb experience as the Japanese survivors of the war felt it and talked about it and prayed about it.

The Mayor of Hiroshima Hamai Shinzo spoke, the U.S. Ambassador to Japan - Edwin Reischauer of Harvard - spoke, representatives of the *hibakusha*, the survivors, spoke, and there was an hypnotic droning over the loud speakers of Japanese Buddhist chanting throughout the ceremony. At precisely 08:16, during the Moment of Silence, a flock of doves was released - they were actually pigeons, even if some of them were all white - and they flew up into the air over the Peace Park. It was very dramatic and heart-rending, representing as it did the expression, the profound expression, of a desire for world peace. Then, the Mayor read the names of the roughly 400 persons who had died in the preceding 12 months of what were called A-bomb-related diseases.

The problem was that it is impossible to say with any certainty in any given case whether the disease was produced by the radiations from the A-bomb, because there was no signature disease that was produced by the A-bomb. If someone died of leukemia and had been heavily exposed close to the epicenter, perhaps it was reasonable to call his or her leukemia A-bomb related, leukemia was a known effect on humans of ionizing radiations; but there was no proof or certainty in an individual case. I supposed that it did not matter much, and why not enable such "*hibakusha*" to obtain benefits from the Government? But, still, the numbers got beefed up that way and lacked a certain scientific basis in fact.

Nonetheless, I thought to myself, so many people died at the moment of the explosion, and people were still dying, I supposed, from their exposures. Perhaps it was a worthwhile thing to come to this City dedicated to Peace to keep alive the memories of those who have died as well as to understand how many are continuing to die these twenty years later and of what. I became gradually convinced that it was well worth a major portion of my (scientific) life to document the later effects of the ionizing radiations since I was somewhat uniquely now in a position to apply the latest technology in genetics to the studies of the hibakusha.

After the reading of the names by Mayor Hamai – reminding me of the Yizkor Service of Remembrance on Yom Kippur in my Synagogue at home – and after the tolling of the Buddhist bells in the Peace Park I approached the cenotaph where the names of the 400 would be added to the already 140,000 names of those who had died at the time of the bombings and over the following 20 years. The cenotaph was a simple concrete chamber covered by a saddle-shaped monument designed by Kenzo Tange, the renowned Japanese architect. There was a permanent or eternal flame, first lit two years earlier in 1964, with an inscription saying, in translation, we shall not repeat the evil of war. I have never been sure who the "we" was referring to – the Japanese? the peoples of the world? In any event I was very moved by the rituals and ceremony, which gave me serious pause to think about why I was in Hiroshima, what I was meant to do there.

From the Cenotaph, I wandered under Iida-san's tutelage, to the Children's Peace Monument, dedicated to the children who died on August 6, 1945, as well as to those children who had died since of suspected A-bomb diseases. There was a carved statue of a young girl with arms outstretched and the image of a folded paper crane in her hand. She represented Sasaki Sadako, a young teenage girl who developed leukemia soon after the bombing. The story goes that Sadako believed that if she folded 1000 paper cranes she would be cured. She died before she could finish but, supposedly, her classmates took up her challenge and completed the 1000 cranes in her honor. Ever since, it has become a ritual among elementary school children in Hiroshima and throughout Japan to fold paper cranes in Sadako's memory.

From the *Heiwa Koen*, the Peace Park, and from most everywhere in Hiroshima, the skeletal remains of the Hiroshima Industrial Promotion Hall are visible as a rounded Dome, the only building left standing in any shape in Hiroshima City after the A-bomb explosion. As I subsequently learned during my years in Hiroshima, maintaining the A-bomb Dome was a regular part of the City's budget and a not inconsequential and much debated expense at that, especially for a rebuilding city. Its preservation as a symbol was worth a great deal and so it was funded each year, but not without occasional controversy.

What surprised me most of all, was that Hiroshima Day was a very active commercial day in the City, with shopkeepers trying hard to induce passers-by to come in to shop, eat, browse. I had this misbegotten image of a very quiet almost sacred 24 hours in the A-bombed City on August 6th, but such was not at all the case. There was, after the ceremony at the Peace Park, a festive atmosphere that seemed to this alien a kind of sacrilege. But, Iida-san told me it was "normal" and no disrespect was intended, the merchants were for the most part people who had entered the City after the blast and so for them, most of them, the commercial activities were untainted by personal or sentimental values.

That evening, however, there was a very moving ceremony - even for the new merchant class - on the Ota River in the City center: candles were mounted on small wooden bases, enshrouded with rice paper frames and sent off downstream one by one until the river was a sea of floating, lit candles, representing the last journey of the spirits of the dead. It was mostly a silent ceremony, except for some Buddhist chanting, and a very moving sight. Especially when one recalled how many seared men, women and children had found refuge in the Ota River to cool their burnt flesh right after the A-bomb blast and in the first days thereafter.

7

The Atomic Bomb Casualty Commission: ABCC

The Hibakusha

Iida-san and I got down to the serious business of establishing the cytogenetics laboratory at ABCC, essentially using the methods I had learned at the NIH in Hin Tjio's lab. We quickly put into place the techniques of cell culture, the harvesting of dividing cells, and the chromosomal analysis under the microscope and via black and white photography. Iida-san was fortunately skillful with the camera lens on the microscope and with reproduction of sharply focused images of chromosomes for analysis, as we wanted to document our findings in detail.

We planned to study the blood cell chromosomes of: a) those people directly exposed to the radiations from the bomb, at a range of doses - largely correlated with distance from the hypocenter - from those close in and heavily exposed to those farther out and basically unexposed; b) those people who were exposed in utero, i.e., those whose mothers were exposed while pregnant with them; and c) those who had one or both parents exposed but who were themselves conceived after the exposure. This latter group was the so-called F1 generation, and from a genetic point of view was particularly important because future generations needed to know if they were likely to inherit chromosomal mutations, or other mutations for that matter. And the F1's were stigmatized in Japanese society as almost untouchables in terms of marriageability.

We studied the first two groups for evidence of cellular abnormalities that might predispose them to cancer, for example, or birth defects when they elected to have children. There were large scale population studies - epidemiological studies - being simultaneously conducted on these populations for any increases in cancers or other diseases, but our chromosome studies would represent direct biological evidence in individuals of cellular genetic damage if we were to find any. As such it was critically important to the survivors, their children and the scientific world to know if such damage could be shown.

We worked long and hard on these studies, added several people to our staff because the volume of work was huge; but we did not forget to have an occasional celebratory *saki* and/or dinner downtown after our long days in the lab. We went to bars and restaurants where we became well known. One of my favorites was the Kanzashi, a ten-seat tempura bar with a taste that was beyond description, the shrimp and vegetables being served on skewers, and the cost being determined by the number of skewers consumed.

It was not an inexpensive restaurant, but my boss at ABCC, Dr Howard Hamilton, the Director of Clinical Labs, was a favorite of the sensei's, who shared Howard's love for Noh Drama. At the Kanzashi, I was mad for the quail eggs, briefly deep fried in the Master's batter which only he could create. Further, I became an afficionado of sashimi and sushi in a series of joints that stayed open late into the night – the Suishin was for family meals but there were many so-called unnamed four- or five-person stand bars where gentlemen could, late at night, consume gobs of sushi while also consuming gobs of saki. Hiroshima being by the Inland Sea the fish were fresh and delicious.

There were also innumerable *yakiniku* (beef) restaurants where the specially flavored meats were also served on skewers, deliciously and delicately flavored beef of Kobe or Matsuzaka origin. The best of Japanese cows were fed beer and had their flesh hand massaged, resulting in a beautifully marbled meat that fairly melted in the mouth.

These taste treats enabled us to work hard and do what was necessary over the next couple of years to see what could be found from the chromosomal point of view.

Basically, among the exposed A-bomb survivors we found, even 20 years after exposure, that there were indeed breaks and rearrangements of the chromosomes in the blood cells of the *hibakusha*; that the numbers were proportional to the radiation exposure doses; and that some of these abnormalities reproduced or cloned themselves, so that one might find multiple cells from the same individual with the identical abnormality.

It was unsure what the biological significance of these

breaks was, but the assumption had to be that this induced damage was deleterious and adversely affected the normality and survival of the cells. It also by inference suggested that the same types of abnormalities were probably induced in other tissues beside the blood cells, perhaps leading to cancers in these other organs: that was unproven but was a reasonable scientific hypothesis. Very important findings. We published them in the scientific literature after presenting the data at various meetings in Japan, and even back in Washington at a specially convened meeting of the U.S. National Academy of Sciences which oversaw the ABCC Program.

Among those exposed in utero, i.e., when their mothers were pregnant with them, we noted that the only significant clinical finding in them as a group was small head circumference, though importantly this reduced head circumference was really more of a statistical finding than a clinical one, given that the individuals so tainted were of normal IQ and life expectancy. However, we did find, in a small sample of in utero exposed, similar kinds of chromosomal aberrations as in the post-natally exposed survivors. Again, in the apparent absence of clinical abnormality. No increase in leukemia or other cancers was noted in the very small group of in utero exposed that was known to us. This was an important finding in that it meant that whatever clinical effect these aberrations of the chromosomes might have the magnitude of the effect was very low- a useful, reassuring fact that emerged from this work. To be sure, the total number of in utero exposed was only 1600, so development of cancers could be expected to be very infrequent.

In a similar vein the hibakusha and the scientific world awaited the F1 findings, as by the time we got there one might well have expected genetic effects to have become manifest, it being a full generation after the A-bomb exposure. We knew that the F1 would be a complex study because several factors could combine to lower the probability of our finding anything. First, the principal was different from direct observation of damage to the somatic, or non-germ cells, in the survivors themselves: In the F1 study we were searching *indirectly* for damage to the germ cells of exposed parents. Thus, damage would have had to be induced in the genetic material of exposed mothers or fathers; said damage would have had to be non-lethal to the functioning of the germ cells; would have had to survive conception AND would have had to have been transmitted to a viable conceptus or offspring as well. Numerous *ifs*, numerous points at which a damaged strand of DNA could have failed to replicate or failed to have been passed along in a viable form.

We elected to identify a subset of children/offspring whose fathers were exposed; or whose mothers were exposed; or both of whose parents were exposed; as well as a subset (controls) neither of whose parents were exposed. And, of course, the parents would have been exposed over a range of doses. In these offspring we were looking for the presence of extra chromosomes, as in Down's syndrome, as well as the presence of stable rearrangements of the chromosomes that could appear in the survivor parent's sperm cells or ova, survive gamete or germ cell formation, as well as conception itself and then appear in the F1 child at birth.

With these provisos we pressed ahead and did what we

could to see if there were any transmissible cytogenetic effects demonstrable in the F1 generation. In sum – and crucially for both the offspring and their parents - there were not. At that time – given the techniques we had available to us - we found no genetic damage in the children of exposed parents.

This enabled that generation to marry and reproduce a bit more freely than it otherwise would have. There were caveats we could not eliminate; but on the whole, there were no gross F1 effects that we could detect. That did not mean that there were no effects – it simply meant that we could not demonstrate any effect.

With the work proceeding well, and with our findings of considerable interest to both the community of survivors and to the medical/scientific community worldwide, I was invited to present the findings widely throughout Japan, primarily at meetings of the Japanese Society of Human Genetics, as well as to the National Academy of Sciences in Washington, and other medical and radiation societies around the world. Articles followed in the press. Perhaps my two most noteworthy presentations and trips were to the International Society of Hematologists – which was meeting in Sydney, Australia – and to an international symposium on Human Radiation Cytogenetics at Western General Hospital in Edinburgh, Scotland, where a distinguished cadre of radiation cytogeneticists had worked for years on patients who had had radiation therapy for ankylosing spondylitis, a serious often debilitating disease of the spine. The Edinburgh Group was very intimidating, but very important, and having their blessing on our work was crucial to our credibility internationally. And so, after presenting our findings in Sydney at the Hematology Meeting - the first international medical conference ever held in Australia - I flew to Edinburgh into the lions' den, where Professor Court Brown and his austere minions awaited me. They were especially prepared because numerous articles about our findings had appeared in the Australian and other international presses. They did not know me and they did not believe the press reports to which they had access.

I shall always remember my arrival in frigid, dark Edinburgh late that October (1966), friendless and largely unknown but awaited. The Edinburgh group, led by Michael Court Brown and staffed by Karin Buckton, Patricia Jacobs - who went on to have a particularly outstanding career in cytogenetics - David Harnden and others had demonstrated chromosomal abnormalities in the blood cells of the spondylitics who had had radiation therapy and an increase in leukemias, somewhat analogous to our studies in the Hiroshima and Nagasaki survivors, though a different type of radiation at high doses only. I presented the Hiroshima and Nagasaki data we had accumulated over the first year of our work and assuaged the cynicism that the newspaper reports had generated. Our laboratory was now "on the map" and our findings would be followed in the next years with great interest by the genetics community.

I noted with some shock a couple of years later that Professor Court Brown himself died at age 50, in 1972, a serious loss to the radiation cytogenetics community and the laboratory he had built. He was a co-editor of the book which resulted from the 1966 Conference, entitled *Human Radiation*

Cytogenetics: Proceedings of an International Symposium in Edinburgh, October 1966 (with Hugh Evans and Angus McLean, published by the North-Holland Press in 1967), a seminal work as the new field of human cytogenetics took hold.

While I was returning to Hiroshima from Edinburgh a flock of geese flew into one of the engines of my British Airways flight, and so we landed in Frankfort to await a replacement plane. The BA staff loaded the passengers onto buses and we spent a day in the Black Forest and towns outside of Munich consuming large quantities of Bavarian beer – a passion easily developed.

I worked hard in the months after the Edinburgh conference to see to the development of the Cytogenetics Laboratory of the Nagasaki Branch of the ABCC. I had been to Nagasaki several times during the first year in Japan and loved the city and its contrast with Hiroshima. People seemed gentler and the pace of life was slower. Being a largely mountainous area around central Nagasaki City, the A-bomb that exploded there on August 9th, 1945, struck in an odd way, with many people protected by the intervening mountains from the radiations of Fat Man's gamma radiations. Fat Man was a plutonium bomb and released more radioactivity into the environment than did the uranium bomb Big Boy in Hiroshima. About 40,000 people died directly from the bombing in Nagasaki. But with the radiation sickness, leukemia and other cancers that followed, the estimate is that over-all some 80,000 people died at or in the aftermath of the explosion.

From the beginning of the ABCC an attempt was made

to implement the same studies in Nagasaki as in Hiroshima. Though there were fewer exposed in Nagasaki the effort was important because the types of radiations differed, yet the social stigma attached to the exposures was similar. And, there was much to be learned from the thousands of people who were exposed to what was primarily the gamma radiation of the plutonium bomb dropped on Nagasaki.

Our cytogenetic work was done using the same methods in both cities, and the findings were similar: dose-response relationships, clones of mutant cells with the same abnormality, chromosomal aberrations in the blood cells of the in utero exposed, and nil in the F1's.

The key player in Nagasaki for me was a pediatrician-cum-geneticist named Shotaro Neriishi. He had been at Nagasaki ABCC for several years before I arrived in Japan, doing clinical examinations on the F1's mainly. But he was interested in the chromosome studies, was very open to learning the new methods and to developing the laboratory there in tandem with our group in Hiroshima. In a sense, I was his sensei in the laboratory and he was my sensei in all other matters Japanese, not only but especially as relates to Nagasaki, his native place. We became dear friends as well as colleagues, and together we built the lab there. All the while he guided me over much of Japan.

In Nagasaki Neriishi-sensei and I spent time at the Monument to the 26 Catholic Martyrs, who were forced to carry their crosses on their backs in 1597, as they made their way to Nagasaki down from Kyoto and Osaka. Nagasaki was open to Christianity over the years, though it was outlawed by the Tokugawa regime in the 17th century in most of the rest of the country. The Oura Church was a small wooden church built as a monument to those Catholic Martyrs.

Neriishi-sensei guided me patiently each time I visited the laboratory in Nagasaki, from place to place: the Glover Tei (House) home of the Scotsman Thomas Glover on whom the "Madame Butterfly" character was said to be based. The view of Nagasaki Harbor from that house was gorgeous. We went to the Urakami Cathedral which was destroyed by the A-bomb but rebuilt in the 1950's. I was very interested in the long history of Chinese Buddhism in Nagasaki and we visited the Sofuku-ji Temple which was/is, arguably, the best representation of Chinese architecture in all of Japan.

Kyushu has many hot spas and several volcanos and Neriishi-sensei saw to my travels to Mount Unzen, where I hiked with him to the rim of the heavily sulfurous volcano, and to Mount Aso, the largest active volcano in Japan with hot springs which relaxed us in the evening and led me into a deeper feeling about the Zen way.

As time passed I came to value my days in Nagasaki with Dr Neriishi and then gradually with his wife and family who welcomed me – as well as my own family – into their home. One evening Neriishi-sensei made more of a fuss than usual to have me to his home – and after a few minutes of chatting with his family, he reappeared in kimono (formal robes) and led me, my wife, and his wife to another room, where he had set up to perform the Tea Ceremony in my honor. He wore a dark kimono, and handled the whisk and the bowls with an elegance I had never seen, stirring the green paste into the bowls of hot water in a finely prescribed way. He liked and studied the Tea Ceremony for its very slowness and peacefulness, traits some find maddening but which I came to respect and admire.

He and I had our favorite haunts, especially nocturnal haunts, in Nagasaki. I adored the food in the city, especially the sashimi. He led the way to almost all of the best restaurants, especially those with "living fish", fish and shellfish swimming around in huge tanks, plucked out of the water and served immediately, responding to a drop of saki by contracting on the plate before us or even in the *hashi* (chopsticks) as we held the fish poised to eat them. The world of very good tastes made my trips to Nagasaki a pleasure.

Following the feasts of fish and marvelous Chinese food as well, we would go to a club or two, where the young ladies came to know us in that superficial way bar girls in Japan helped visitors spend an occasional evening. Harmless evenings of fun and pleasure. After the nightclubs, we favored a particular stand-bar, the Chanel 5, in the center of the city, a small bar with perhaps nine or ten seats, with a woman about 50, the owner, who served as hostess and kept us entertained with her stories of times past. Mme Kii-san was an ex-geisha, Neriishi-sensei explained to me, who had a patron, probably a former lover, who, upon her retirement from the profession, had set her up with this bar as a source of income and enjoyment. Neriishi-sensei and I frequented the Chanel 5 whenever we could, and I came to understand that my visits to Nagasaki provided us both with an opportunity to have these nights out on the town, eating, drinking and gently carousing.

One memorable evening, Motomichi Tomonaga, a distinguished internist-hematologist in the Department of

Medicine at Nagasaki University, gave a reception in my honor at a beautiful inn/restaurant high on a hill overlooking Nagasaki Harbor. Attending were muck-a-mucks from the Prefectural Office and others from Nagasaki University. Tomonaga–sensei was a superb hematologist/internist who worked closely with the A-bomb survivors. He and I liked one another and had become good friends during my early months in Japan.

We were fed utterly delectable fresh fish from Nagasaki Bay, and were entertained by maiko-sans, apprentice geishas, overseen by several older geishas, skilled in the arts of samisen-playing, dancing and conversation. One of the geishas, a certain Nobuko, was obviously assigned to pay special attention to me as the Guest of Honor. She was well attired in a gorgeous silk kimono embroidered with butterflies, and her skin was whitened with powders and scents. Her coiffure was that of a classical geisha, a traditional headdress from the time of Lady Murasaki. I was enchanted, transported back to earlier times.

Somehow, I got it into my head that I would like to see Nobuko-san after the party either later that evening or the next day. Nobuko-san did agree, to everyone's surprise to have tea with me at the European-style Gin Rei Restaurant the next day at 3 pm. Dr. Nerishii agreed to serve as chaperone, in what I knew he felt was a risky business, risky for Nobuko, for me and for him as well, all our reputations being at stake.

I was unsure whether Nobuko would show up, given the potential damage to her reputation as one of Nagasaki's finest Geishas, but meet the next day we did, despite her trepidations. She was a brave soul to have come, but once having said she would she was obliged.

She turned out to be a thirtyish-year old woman, with close-cropped short hair of a peculiar brownish tint – as many women in Japan had in those days – and a pleasant face. If you passed her in the street you would not take particular notice. But she was very personable. We talked via Neriishi–sensei about the weather, her upcoming dental appointment, and the health of her aging parents with whom she lived. She asked about my family, especially my two daughters whose pictures I showed her from my wallet. After an hour or so, she excused herself and departed the Gin Rei – the end of an episode that I engineered, wisely or unwisely. I was adventurous in those ways and rarely regretted it, but such doings could be a bit unwise for all.

Neriishi-sensei and I had serious business together, and I remain grateful to him for what he did on that front. In his quiet way he urged me to meet and interact with the major figures in Japan in pediatrics and in genetics. I did this under his tutelage by going to meetings, making contact with leaders in these fields in Tokyo, Kyoto, Osaka and, of course, in Hiroshima. I made pediatric rounds at Hiroshima University Hospital with Professor Kazuo Otani, the chairman of pediatrics. I was intent on learning about Japanese academia and the practice of pediatrics.

Each Monday I would appear on the pediatrics ward, look over the charts of the newly arrived patients – written in Japanese, German and English by the resident staff – and then Professor Otani would lead about fifteen of us to the bedsides for case presentations. At first I was perturbed by these Rounds: there was no discussion as I had become accustomed to at Hopkins. I was used to lengthy considerations at the bedside or in the hallways about differential diagnoses and possible treatment courses. But, here in Hiroshima, Professor Otani would listen to the case history, as presented by one of the resident physicians; would then examine the patient and give us the diagnosis, treatment plan, etc, immediately after which we would move on as a group to the next patient. One of his staff members took copious notes as the Professor spoke. If for example a patient had an elevated white count with an increase in the granulocytic type of white blood cells, Professor Otani would simply say this was a classic case of childhood leukemia, requiring thus and such chemotherapy for x duration. End of story. If I dared to raise the possibility of infectious or other causes for the elevated white cell count, it was not appreciated and not discussed,

This was the Japanese or at least the Hiroshima way of medicine at the time, copied largely from German and other European cultures, in which the one full professor in the department determined all, from positions to salaries to diagnoses. I tried for a while, largely because I liked Professor Otani very much on a personal level, but I much preferred the open discussion of possible diagnoses and treatments to which I was accustomed in the States. I was impatient with the Otani Way and so I stopped attending these weekly rounds after several months. But I felt very good that Professor Otani had welcomed me and went out of his way to make me feel a part of his group. I tried not to insult him with my departure, but I had become "too busy" to carry on.

Meanwhile a major decision had to be made about the cytogenetics labs in Hiroshima and Nagasaki. I was scheduled to work in Japan for two years and had been there one year already, but in these U.S. governmental matters, one had to plan ahead. That was especially true vis-à-vis overseas assignments. But of even more importance was the very future of the work. In one year we had really just begun, and I surely did not want the studies to stop with my departure scheduled for a year later.

I had enjoyed living in Hiroshima, even as an alien scientist affiliated with the U.S. Government. I had begun to think perhaps I would stay on a while. My U.S. PHS supervisor Al Hilberg came out from Washington from time to time to see how we were doing - and to enjoy himself - and when I told him of the possibility I might stick around a while, he put his hand on my shoulder and said, "Arthur, you know I hope, that if you stay too long people (in Washington) will begin to wonder about you?" I knew there was plenty of gossip about the small group of Americans who stayed for years at ABCC - Howard, Hamilton, Chief of Clinical Labs; Walter Russell, Chief of Radiology; et alia - and I hated that stuff: why were they there? what were they running from? Even, by implication, their sexual orientation was questioned? While I cared not at all what people thought of me (or them) in this regard, nobody's business but their own, I was very annoyed to think such questions might be raised about me by my staying on another few years. Ridiculous.

But the cytogenetic studies had implications that went well beyond my personal feelings. And I was committed to leaving a program that was self-sustaining and not dependent on my presence. Dr. Neriishi had introduced me at one of the meetings of the Japanese Society of Genetics to a certain Professor Sajiro Makino from Hokkaido University. In true Japanese fashion, Professor Makino ran the best department of genetics in all of Japan, and the only one seriously devoted to the study of chromosomes. Dr. Neriishi informed me that Professor Makino was going to retire in a few years, and upon his retirement he had to have placed all his students and faculty in other departments around the country, no easy matter, but as Professor that was his duty.

For our part, we had decided that we could accommodate several additional senior geneticists - four or five - over the next few years between the growing Hiroshima and Nagasaki labs. So, Dr Neriishi and I flew on All Nippon Airways from Hiroshima to Tokyo Haneda and from there to Sapporo in Hokkaido, where we had arranged to meet with Professor Makino. I was filled with anxiety as this interview was important for the future of our program.

Professor Sajiro Makino was a scientist much like then Emperor Hirohito: that is, he had multiple interests, with his being the future of his staff - he was retiring in two years - and the breeding of prize-winning chrysanthemums. He showed me his blossoms with great pride, large, pure colored blooms, polyploid organisms much larger than the usual chrysanthemum grown in hothouses around the country.

Our discussion of the work in Hiroshima and Nagasaki involved his Associate Professor Dr Motomichi Sasaski, who knew and guided the work and interests of the younger staff of the Chromosome Research Unit very well. We reviewed in detail the nature of our F1, in utero exposed and Adult Health Study findings and then discussed the possibility of Professor Makino coming to Hiroshima for a visit in the weeks ahead to see first-hand the facilities and meet the director of ABCC, Dr George Darling, as well as the Japanese National Instititutes of Health Associate Director who led the Japanese side of the work, Dr Hiroshi Maki. Nerishii-sensei and I toured Professor Makino's Laboratory and were introduced to the junior staff of younger, eager and very smart investigators.

We left Sapporo that evening, elated that Professor Makino was sufficiently interested to make a trip to Hiroshima. After complex negotiations in the next weeks, and a series of complex arrangements for housing during his stay and for a grand dinner in his honor at the Iwaso Ryokan, Dr Makino did come with Associate Professor Sasaki. By a curious twist of fate Professor Makino's mentor, an elderly scientist of renown in silkworm genetics, one Sakamoto-sensei, had retired from Tokyo University to his original birthplace in Hiroshima. We invited Professor Sakamoto to the dinner, thus effecting the reunion of the two deans of Japanese genetics, an event for which Professor Makino was very grateful.

Professor Makino had, then, in his power to provide high quality staff to our program to continue what we had started. I felt strongly that finding Japanese staff instead of American staff was infinitely better, as the transient use of two-year people was by definition impermanent whereas the Japanese who came down from Sapporo could well provide a long-term solution and ensure the continuity we wanted. Since my own "tour" was up in some months, Professor Makino sagely asked if I would be willing to extend another year, to see to the adjusting of his people into the American-run program. I had to think about that long and hard since I was preparing to leave soon for the States, and this would extend me, and my family, a third year. Not a great sacrifice as we loved being there, I especially, and my willingness to extend would serve as a statement of faith to Professor Makino. Furthermore, there was really no rush to get back, as I was at the start of my academic career, and another year more or less mattered to no one.

I discussed with my seniors at ABCC and especially with my Washington Public Health Service bosses, who paid me. All were in agreement that for the sake of the continuity of the program I could/should stay.

With that I thought how very lucky we were to live in the Kamotani-tei, Kamotani House, just on the outskirts of Hiroshima City in the village of Takasu, a streetcar stop about three miles from the center of Hiroshima City. Mme Kamotani, whose house this was, had rented the house out to the ABCC which, in turn, assigned it and their other real estate interests, to ABCC staff. But the Kamotani House was a special place: I loved it then and I have loved the memories of it to this day.

The house was surrounded by a wall like most private homes of its generation in Japan, so passers-by could not look in. The wall also surrounded the formal Japanese gardens of Kamotani-tei, with the copious azalea bushes and the pond for *koi* (prized carp), where I used to sit and also walk for many hours. The house itself had three large 12-mat tatami rooms, two on the main floor with *fusuma* doors in between the two rooms and sliding glass doors abutting the corridor that circumnavigated the entire tatami mat complex. There was also a westernized kitchen and a hard-floor reception room. Upstairs, the master bedroom was a mirror-image of the large tatami room below it, with a similar creaking wood floor surrounding it. There were two bedrooms for the children also on the second floor, to keep them close to their parents.

ABCC recommended to us an *amah,* a nanny, called Toda-san, a substantial and very gentle older woman from Nagasaki who came up to work with us. Toda-san was devoted to the care and nurturing of our two little girls, both under five. I have to this day a mental image of Mme Toda as *Le Coeur Simple* of Flaubert - a person who in many ways, in the simplicity of her devotion, was a beautiful soul. I am under no illusions about Toda-san: she may or may not have felt the affection in which she was held - though she surely felt it from my younger daughter. Toda–san had served as amah to many ABCC families before us and we were to be her last, so her affection was undoubtedly spread a bit thin, but all very manageable. When we finally did leave Japan after three years, Toda-san went back to Nagasaki and kept in touch with us only rarely, as her English writing skills were far less developed than her oral skills. But her memory has been happily preserved by us over the years.

Toward the end of my first two years in Hiroshima I was strolling one April day in the Takasu area where the kamotani-tei was located, enjoying the blooms on the cherry blossom trees, when I met a young Japanese woman from nearby Kure. She turned out to be a graduate student at Hiroshima University in literature and languages, name of Matsunaga Sachiko. She was heading for a nearby coffee shop, and invited me along so she could practice her English conversation. For her the invitation may have been to practice her English, but for me it was other.

Sachiko was tall for a Japanese woman, maybe five foot six or seven, with long tresses of jet black hair falling below her shoulders and well down her back. Shades of Murasaki, I thought to myself. Her skin was olive-complected, soft and silk-like to the observer, and her smile was gentle and sweet as was her voice. She was not as shy as the average Japanese woman in the presence of a *gaijin* (foreigner), at least based on my experience to that point, an experience in which the word *hazukashi* (the Japanese expression for shyness) featured prominently. No, Sachiko had asked me to join her for the coffee - in itself a rare expression of daring - and then asked me lots of questions about myself and my life in Japan and in the U.S. For my part, I asked where she was now living - she had a room in a private home in nearby Furue - and what her daily life was like as a student albeit a graduate student in languages at *Hirodai* (Hiroshima University). We spent a pleasant hour together, and agreed to meet again at the coffee shop later that week.

As time went on we met at the coffee shop, occasionally at the Miyajima Shrine on the Inland Sea for longer strolls and talks, or in downtown Hiroshima. We talked for hours on end usually, and through her I learned much about Japan. I also learned about the fate of her family and friends after the

A-bomb explosion. It was an education to know this perceptive young woman whose family had suffered much: they lost their home on the outskirts of Hiroshima; her father had suffered excruciating back burns and remained badly scarred; and her mother had recently developed acute leukemia from which she would later die.

I was admittedly very attracted to Sachiko. Making love to a Lady Murasaki surrogate had been a dream. And I thought long and hard about the wisdom of our having a sexual relationship - which I did feel was possible. I did not really know how Sachiko would feel about this , but the signals - the touching of hands over a cup of coffee, her invitations from time to time for meetings in out of the way places, her never saying no to any of my proposed get-togethers - led me to believe she felt similarly inclined. However, I was a family man and soon to return to the U.S. And for Sachiko involvement with a gaijin would have been very unwise, a non-removable stain.

8

More of Life in Japan

Hiroshima and Nagasaki

In late 1964, prior to embarking for Hiroshima, I heard on the radio in Baltimore a beautiful, exotic-sounding Concerto for Koto and Orchestra, played by one Kimio Eto with the Philadelphia Symphony Orchestra. The Concerto was written by Henry Cowell whose music I did not know, but the orchestra was led that evening by Leopold Stokowski, so I decided to listen on. As I listened I decided that if the occasion ever arose I would try to learn to play this extraordinary instrument called the koto.

Once in Japan, I developed a serious interest in it. I started to play this thirteen - stringed instrument of hollowed out pawlonia wood that one sat on the floor to pluck with finger picks. The tone emitted from the wood depended to some extent on the grain of the wood used, such that the parabolic patterns of the grain went from broad strokes to small parabolas that delivered a beautiful, harp-like quality of sound and I loved it. The koto masters in Japan were almost all blind and so the music itself was transmitted orally and aurally from master to student. However. while the masters were blind – the better to hear the subtleties of the notes? - the teachers were for the most part sighted women like my teacher Tsugi-san, who had her own school of perhaps twenty students, all women, except for the occasional *gaijin* like me. Once a year her students would gather for their annual concert, at which all students at all levels played in harmony – or disharmony – the classical pieces in the repertoire, pieces like *Rokudan* and *Sakura* and others more complex. We played together and, selectively, individually. I have never been so tense and frankly panicked as when I had, after a year of weekly lessons, to play a piece on my own at the annual concert. Draped in my new simple black kimono with the cedar tree as my chosen crest, I sat on the tatami, my recently acquired koto on the mat in front of me, as I stumbled through Rokudan. Much worse a panic than when at 13 I had tried to play my trumpet one night in Nantasket Beach at the community social hall and I split the first six notes of Vaughn Monroe's "Dance, Ballerina, Dance."

I became seriously interested in reading about classical Japanese music, from the numerous versions of the koto – three strings to 17 – as well as the bamboo *shakuhachi* flute, the three-stringed *shamisen* and the ancient *biwa*. At the Maruzen Bookstore in downtown Hiroshima there were several though not many texts on ethnomusicology involving Japanese music, but I could find none devoted to explicating the music itself of the koto with which I was passionately in love. And so, I resolved to do a book which dealt in detail with the many pieces of koto music with which Tsugi–san was teaching me.

Word reached me that one of the secretaries to my koto-playing associate Walter Russell in Radiology was a serious kotoist and a serious young woman. I met with Michiko Hamaoka-san to discuss my idea for the book and she agreed to meet with me once each week at noon on her lunch break to begin the process of outlining our magnum opus tentatively entitled, "Music of the Koto."

Hamaoka-san as a friend was a revelation. Unlike Sachiko, Hamaoka-san was always very formal with me as we worked on transposing the Japanese music of the pentatonic scale onto Western style notation, with sharps and flats, codas, and staffs, quarter notes and half-notes, etc. We discussed the origins of her interest in the koto, and Hamaoka-san explained to me that like most young Japanese women she had begun studying two things when she was very young: flower arranging – in the Ikebana school – and koto playing. Her parents had insisted that those were the two arts every Japanese girl had to learn. Which meant studying them year after year throughout their youth and adolescence, and on into maturity. These were the two classical fields of expertise every young woman had to master to become a proper wife, she explained to me. True, some studied the three - stringed shamisen played with a plectrum; some studied Japanese dance. But those were more to entertain guests than thc koto playing was, and they were less suitable for development of the proper young woman, which Hamaoka-san's parents were seeing to in their daughter.

From our weekly meetings I learned much respect for this woman, as I came to understand the delicacy and the gentility of the Japanese woman of a certain station. She stood about five foot five, wore Western-style clothes at all times to her job at ABCC, and was always well - coiffed. She was shy and it took months before she could bring herself to ask me about my life before Japan, about my family, about life in the United States but thought it impolite to ask. She wanted to know about all such matters and so I talked little by little about these things with her after our sessions on the koto book. In a sense that was her reward for the hours spent putting up with my endless questions about the origins of the music we both loved. The contact was a bit of glue between us.

I recognized that Hamaoka-san was very attractive and I was drawn to her in a respectful way. I came to understand that she was a brave young woman for doing the book with me, as she was inevitably gossiped about at the ABCC because of her relationship with me and the time spent alone with me, proper as it was. I decided therefore to put neither her nor myself in any social jeopardy. The risk for a young woman in her position of being known as a friend to a young American - or by implication, perhaps more than a friend - was simply too great and had to be handled with the greatest of care. We remained colleagues doing a book together on music we both loved. That was the fact, but facts have never stopped a good gossip from spreading rumors which did happen though with no adverse results that I knew of.

Some years after my departure I learned that Hamaoka-san had married a doctor from Nagasaki, and had a son soon thereafter. We exchanged letters occasionally over the years, though we never did finish the koto book.

One of my greatest pleasures while living in Hiroshima was working with my very sophisticated, multi-talented boss at ABCC, Howard Hamilton, who was Chief of Clinical Laboratories. Howard grew up in Lake Forest, Illinois; went to Columbia for medical school; and trained in pediatrics at the Massachusetts General Hospital. Howard began his life in Japan as an Army doctor, assigned to Tokyo and environs during the Occupation. He came to like Japan so much during his Army time that once his two - year tour was up, he decided to stay on if he could. He somehow arranged to go to work for the U.S. National Academy of Sciences which ran the Atomic Bomb Casualty Commission. He had been living in Japan for perhaps ten years by the time I arrived in the mid-1960's.

But he was not really incorporated into the social fabric at ABCC, where the wives of staff had created their own modus vivendi, with ABCC cars transporting them to the local U.S. Marine Corps Air Station at Iwakuni nearby for shopping, drinking and eating at the Officers' Club, etc. Howard was a bachelor – there were rumors about a divorce State-side, ergo the settling in Hiroshima, but I never got into any of that with him – he never offered and I never asked. Howard had for years explored ways to get around the Japanese laws about foreigners not having the right to own land or houses, and had finally managed to buy a small but utterly charming Japanese house just outside the center of Hiroshima. His maid-san, an older, very diminutive lady named Kii-san, looked after his house and his meals and helped Howard lead a proper Japanese style life, as Howard very much wanted his life to be. It was a life on tatami, one fueled by saki, vodka when his mother came to town from Lake Forest, and lots and lots of gatherings of his Noh comrades.

Howard had been studying Noh drama and dance for years by the time I arrived, and his Noh sensei, Matsuyama-san, showed off Howard's skills at the dance and in chanting whenever and wherever he could. The culmination of his work each year took place on the stage at Miyajima, the famous shrine marked by the Buddhist gate emerging from the waters of the Inland Sea, perhaps ten miles south of Hiroshima City. Under Iida-san's watchful eye I became very interested in photography and wherever I went in Japan the Nikormat camera was in hand. And so it was that Howard designated me as the official photographer for his Noh performance at Miyajima the spring following my arrival.

The implications of that honorific were significant. First, to satisfy Howard the photos had to be of excellent quality, sharply focused and with proper exposure settings in terms of catching the folds of his kimono as he danced, catching the movements of his fan in midair, reflecting the positions of his masked face as he chanted. To those ends Howard insisted on reviewing the dance in great detail again and again in advance of his performance so I would know what was coming at every moment.

Second, the Miyajima stage was at the end of a runway which traversed the waters (and tides) of the Inland Sea, with the annual Noh Festival there being purposefully scheduled for April each year when the tide at the island was low much of the day, thus allowing the photographer(s) to wade in from the shore of Miyajima Island to a position just below the stage, and fully in the mud, to take close-ups as much as possible. Howard would make an album of the event with hundreds of the photos each year. Miyajima was, then, a piece of hard work for me, though I was appreciative of the honor.

That first time I did the photography for Howard's Noh performance at Miyajma – the Noh drama was "The Fisherman", a piece with witches and wild dances – I waded gamely through the low tide waters in my boots in the April cold, snapping madly, as instructed, at appropriate times, getting close-up after close-up of the beautiful kimonos Howard wore as he danced the lead role. A day to remember for both him and me.

Howard's art was widely known, and culminated for him in performances on the Tokyo Noh stage and in occasional performances in the States, with particularly noteworthy recitals at the Japan Society in New York and the Japan-America Society in Washington, D.C. As able a researcher and collaborator as Howard Hamilton was on studies into the effects of the ionizing radiations in Hiroshima and Nagasaki, the Noh was his first love, a serious artistic accomplishment for anyone let alone an American physician from Lake Forest, Illinois.

Life for me in Hiroshima and Nagasaki was a series of discoveries, in our research, in our daily lives, in our very being. But in essence we were always Americans in a foreign land. and that message was deeply felt mainly because of the many ways the Japanese let us know we were guests and not native sons and daughters. For me the full realization came one cold winter's night as I flew in a U.S. Marine Corps helicopter over the Inland Sea.

The ABCC was loosely affiliated with the U.S. Marine Corps Air Station (MCAS) at nearby Iwakuni, about 40 minutes by car south of Hiroshima. This was at the time of the Vietnam War, when many Marine Corps pilots were going back and forth between Japan and one or another MCAS's in South Vietnam. The pilots and their crews were authorized to bring their families over as far as Japan, with the result that the dependent population at Iwakuni soared. Now, I was the only American-trained pediatrician in reasonable proximity to the base and so the doctor in charge of the Base Hospital asked me if I would be willing to see an occasional pediatric patient and help out at difficult labors and deliveries. I agreed without hesitation and it was a privilege.

On that particular February night in 1967, my telephone rang at home at 3 a.m. The guard on duty at the ABCC facility was on the phone and he informed me that he had just received a call from Iwakuni, asking me to go right away to the Hiroshima Airport where a Marine Corps helicopter would come and pick me up so I could attend at the anticipated difficult birth of the baby of one of the MCAS pilots and his wife. After a moment of panic- and questioning about the validity of the call – I dressed, grabbed my medical bag, and drove in my Datsun Bluebird through the dark of night to the Airport to meet up with my chopper.

The Hiroshima Airport was a smallish airport that serviced mostly propeller planes and prop jets which were then a major mode of transport to and from Tokyo, Osaka, and a few other cities in Japan. At three in the morning the airport was completely dark, not a plane in sight on the runway, not a light on in the Terminal. I immediately heard the sound of the helicopter circling over-head, so I parked my car in the front of the terminal building, climbed the fence onto the runway, and tried to figure out how best to let the pilot of the chopper know that I was there.

I remembered back to World War II when the threat of German bombers was real in Boston, so we blacked out the City every night and had patrols walking the streets to make sure everyone's lights were out by ten o'clock sharp. I recalled that that night on the runway of the Hiroshima Airport, because I knew it was possible to see even the smallest light from the ground well up into the sky on a dark night, which this was. I frantically began feeling for my book of matches – I smoked a pipe in those days and was never without my matches – and I quickly began lighting the matches as I stood in the middle of the runway at Hiroshima Airport, to try to catch the attention of the chopper pilot, to let him know I was there.

It worked. After a few minutes the helicopter was heading in my direction, with its spotlight targeted on the exact spot where I had been lighting my matches in a feeble show of presence. I of course ran away from that spot as fast as I could to get out of the way of the landing helicopter's rotary blades. Within seconds after the helicopter hit the ground, an alien-looking corpsman in a large helmet with headlight attached and goggles covering his eyes, jumped out of the plane and yelled, over the din of the chopper motor, "Are you the Doc?"

I climbed aboard, put on the ear mufflers as directed, and

off we flew towards Iwakuni – I presumed. Normally, the drive from Hiroshima City to Iwakuni was along a road that ran parallel to the Inland Sea. But that flight of the helicopter was out to sea in between the numerous Islands, including Miyajima of Noh fame, on what was almost surely a more direct route. I, however, was totally disoriented, and the departing words of my ingénue rang in my ears: "Be careful. The Red Chinese may need a geneticist. Don't let them kidnap you!"

Anything was possible, I supposed, but being kidnapped by the Chinese seemed very unlikely, especially as the corpsman, once he spoke, seemed as American as apple pie. On the other hand, the pilot did not speak so with all that headgear on he could well have been Chinese, or anything else.

We arrived at Iwakuni in about twenty minutes, I was driven right to the base hospital, but the infant was dead and resuscitation was impossible. The umbilical cord had a long while before birth strangulated the baby, and all attempts at getting him to breathe and cry had failed. I spoke to the parents, conveyed the situation to them and told them they would doubtless have other children, though they were inconsolable naturally after the loss of their first offspring.

The Base Commander offered to have me flown back to Hiroshima, but I requested a car and driver, which was graciously provided, reclaiming my Datsun at the Hiroshima Airport the following morning.

Leaving Hiroshima to return to the States was one of the most difficult, saddest decisions of my life. Since then I have often gone over the reasons for the departure. Essentially, while my family and I could never be fully integrated, Japan had become part of who I was and I loved it there. But, as an American I could not become a real part of Japanese medicine or society – that was the blessing and the curse of being a foreigner in the Land of the Rising Sun. Further, the work at ABCC was not basic experimental lab work, it was population-based and I desperately wanted to have a laboratory in which we could vary the work as it mandated, with an emphasis on developing in vitro experimental systems that might show direct evidence of chromosomal and genic mutations in response to chemicals and radiations. Further, on a personal level, my curly-headed daughters were taunted at nursery school and in the neighborhood as being "monsters" by their Japanese classmates and "friends" who regarded these strangers as alien. This was intolerable to their mother and to me. No, there was no choice, all things considered: we had to go home.

I had decided to accept a position as Assistant Professor at the University of Michigan in Ann Arbor, but Barton Childs at Hopkins had offered me a position at Hopkins with him. Much as I loved and admired him the job in Ann Arbor – my own lab, well-funded and with colleagues committed almost exclusively to the world of genetics with only a dash of clinical medicine – was a better one for me at the time, and so it was off to the Middle West to live for the first time in our lives.

When about a hundred co-workers, neighbors, schoolmates of my girls, and family friends showed up at Hiroshima Airport to say "Sayonara", I was touched and honored, as were my then wife and two daughters. I knew that I was likely to return from time to time to look in on the genetics work at ABCC, but it was unlikely the family would join me for my trips. Life back in the States was likely to be involving and, well, our thing. There was really no going back to the way life used to be and I knew it. So, Ann Arbor it was, full-tilt.

9

The Ann Arbor Years

Trying to Become a Midwesterner

It is true that returning to one's native country after a serious period of living - actually living - abroad is unavoidably traumatic. In this instance I anticipated a serious welcome from my new colleagues at Michigan, as well as from my Boston family. In that sense we were not disappointed. It was good just to wake up in the morning and hear English all around me: from television and radio, from neighbors, and from coffee shop personnel. While hearing the Japanese language all the time had been exotic and not alien after three years, in returning I still was relieved of the pressure to understand what people around me were saying, let alone feeling, both at work and in the neighborhood and in the bars, sushi and other, that I frequented. But Ann Arbor was a struggle for this Boston guy.

That said, I had paid a preliminary visit to Ann Arbor and had given a seminar in the Department of Human Genetics which would be my professional base at Michigan, were I to accept the Assistant Professorship offer. I very much liked Ann Arbor and the Department. The town was small but charming and the Department was very welcoming, with superb geneticists of many different ilks with whom to share my professional life and from whom I would doubtless learn a great deal about genetics, from viruses, bacteria, and fungi, on up to humans After Hiroshima and life abroad in a non-English-speaking land, Ann Arbor seemed like a superb entrée back into my native country.

A small house was found for us so we would have a place to put our heads upon arrival, and within a few months we found our own home to buy in Ann Arbor for the longer-term. Meantime, my son Robert was born – and the *bris* – the ritual circumcision - was held to the delight of the Boston Family which joined us for the celebratory occasion. That fall my daughters Karen and Michelle entered the Pattengill Elementary School which was just behind our new home, and they quickly made friends.

For my part, I worked with human cells in the laboratory, cloning lymphocytes; taught my brand of genetics to graduate students and medical students; and ran our Department's weekly Genetics Clinic for counseling patients with a family history of genetic diseases. I worked, notably, with a former friend from Hopkins and the U.S. Public Health Service, Roy Schmickel, who had moved to Ann Arbor from the East Coast where he, as I, had trained at Hopkins in Pediatrics and where both he and I had deep roots. Roy and Leigh moved into a suburban house of substance in Ann Arbor, and we went for dinner there from time to time and visited *en famille*, always a pleasure. Plus Roy and I were favorites of the grad students with whom we attended genetics and pediatrics meetings around the country, giving papers about our work and joining the students for dinner, drinking and partying.

Life in Ann Arbor was generally fine: I made many new friends both on the faculty and in the community, several of whom were friends for a lifetime. I had an almost daily lunch with Mike Levine, a professor in Human Genetics whose work was on the genetics of viruses. Mike had his Ph.D. degree from the University of Indiana which had a distinguished program in Molecular Virology, and Mike had, over the years, become a serious leader in the field. I shared Genetics Clinic duties with fellow pediatrician Roy and with Don Rucknagel, an internist, who specialized in hemoglobinopathies, especially sickle cell anemia which afflicted primarily the black community and was consonant with Don's social conscience. Jim Neel, our distinguished Department Chair participated in the Clinic, was in fact founder of it. The research crew in the Department was excellent and we had a large Program Project Grant from the National Institutes of Health to further the Department's work in human genetics: population genetics, the genetics of blood groups, including the newly discovered histocompatibility locus for transplantation, the genetical control of the synthesis of isoenzymes (different forms of the same enzymes), and others. We had excellent graduate students of whom I had my share and of postdoctoral fellows, who applied directly to work with individual investigators. I had Fellows from Japan, then Czechoslovakia, Switzerland as well as the U.S. My first graduate student going for the PhD. was the brilliant Kyoo Wan Choi, a physician-scientist from Seoul National University in Korea. Thus, we had an interesting, eclectic group in our midst.

In our little two-story lab building in front of the main building of the University of Michigan Medical School, in addition to Mike Levine and myself, were Dick Tashian and Bob Krooth, both mainstays of the Department for many years. I was especially fond of Bob Krooth whose interests paralleled my own in cellular genetics. But I was very fond of them both, as colleagues and friends. Bob and I shared a late arrival hour at the lab: I was a 10 a.m. man and he showed up daily at noon. Bob and Dick were bachelors approaching their forties, so what might be called "confirmed". Except that they were not confirmed, gadding about as they did, going to meetings, spending sabbaticals abroad - Denmark was a favorite location as was London - and they were admittedly not averse to hooking up with the occasional woman for short stints. They were partners with another faculty member in ownership and piloting of a small Cessna which they flew from Ann Arbor's private airport.

I served on the Admissions Committee of the Medical School which was interesting to me because the applicants were often of diverse backgrounds and motivations, and the admissions/rejection process itself was often taxing. But, other committees that spanned the breath of the University were still better suited for me. In particular, the Barbour Scholarship Committee reflected my enthusiasm and experience in the Orient: we gave out perhaps six scholarships a year to Asian women for their studies at the University of Michigan in science, medicine, mathematics, art, et alia, with the notion that they would be returning to their home countries after study in the U.S. The Barbour Committee members were smart and diverse in their interests, and the students almost always had complicated life stories.

Perhaps the most rewarding aspect of life on the faculty at Michigan was the access to graduate students of quality. Kyoo Wan Choi was waiting for me just about as I stepped off the plane from Japan. Wan had come from the great Seoul National University and he knew of my work in cytogenetics and lymphocytes. He and I set about trying to clone lymphocytes in vitro as I had assumed, based on multiple cells with the same complex chromosomal markers, we were seeing in vivo among the A-Bomb survivors. This led to a series of experiments, endless experiments, of plating out lymphocytes in Petri-like dishes with microwells to arrive at a distribution of cells on the plates, which would result in at least some wells with a single cell, ergo the beginnings of a clone. We stimulated the cells with chemicals and viruses, especially the Epstein-Barr virus, to make the individual cells go through cell division to give us pure populations of lymphocytes of single cell origin with which we could work, minimizing the normal genetic variation.

I had other graduate students during my years at Michigan, escorting them through the pangs of their theses on lymphocytes, cellular metabolism, gene activation and even early embryonic gene expression. I taught numerous courses on genetics to the group of twenty to thirty students enrolled each year in the Department's offerings, and had the privilege of teaching a block of clinical genetic material in the Human Genetics Course which was required of first-year medical students.

Bob Krooth finally succumbed to the charms – though he

was one of only a few who detected them - of a chic New York psychologist named Diana. They planned a wedding date and married some six months after their relationship began. It was a small private affair at Bob's apartment in Ann Arbor, and he seemed happy, for a while, though that was not to last long. In fact that marriage was to lead to one of the great tragedies of all of our lives.

During my six years in Ann Arbor, I was *offered* faculty positions at seven other universities, including the University of North Carolina at Chapel Hill, the University of Texas at Galveston, the University of California at San Francisco, my medical alma mater New York University, the University of West Virginia at Morgantown, UCLA - Harbor General, the University of Miami, and there were several others that I did not pursue. In each of the seven instances cited, I received, after considerable negotiation, written offers of appointments at the Associate Professor level - I had come to Ann Arbor as Assistant Professor - with tenure, and serious increases in salary above my modest Ann Arbor salary. And I was offered laboratories and clinical responsibilities commensurate with my interests.

Now it may on the surface appear that I was frivolous in these negotiations, but I was not. Professor Neel had made it clear to me that the University of Michigan, represented by him as Chairman of the Department to which I was primarily attached - I also had an appointment in Pediatrics but Human Genetics was my "home" department - would increase my salary significantly and promote me to Associate Professor with tenure largely on the strength of the interest shown in me by other members of the academic world. And so I had to pursue these other expressions of interest if I was to be able to add to my status economically and professionally at Michigan. That was the system and I had to play the game, or sit there at the Assistant Professor level for many years, which some colleagues elected to do.

For me the understandable effect that this mandatory travelling about to explore other institutions of higher education, at flattering invitations from some very able senior people, was to make me feel less settled in Ann Arbor, despite the very good lifestyle there for the family and myself. To be in high demand as a young, well-travelled, much published junior professor in the rapidly expanding world of human genetics, one who related well to graduate and medical students alike, was to put in jeopardy the stability of our life in that splendid university town. I resented this University-induced destabilizing, but had to adapt.

One of my noteworthy collaborations from Ann Arbor was with Dr. Douglas Gilmour at NYU School of Medicine. Douglas was a UK guy with a PhD in Zoology from Cambridge University, who was a Visiting Professor in the Department of Psychiatry at NYU. He was interested as I was in the tainted evidence making the rounds among scientists that psychoactive drugs like the cannabinoids of marijuana caused damage to the chromosomes, much like the kind of damage we had found among the Hiroshima survivors. That was the hard-to-believe theory, and the supporting evidence was not at all convincing. It seemed to us that this kind of morally-based scientific evidence needed countering with good science.

So Douglas and I began a collaboration which took me into New York regularly, and brought Douglas to Ann Arbor for reviews of own our accumulating data. Doug and his wife Sylvia were given digs in the high-rise Washington Square residences of NYU and I would go there from time to time. While the study findings were of interest to other geneticists, I mainly welcomed the excuse to go to New York, where Douglas introduced me personally to pot, and its pleasures, which we occasionally shared. Doug's son David Gilmour was beginning to gain a reputation as a musician, and lead guitar and singer for the Pink Floyd. He soon thereafter bought Douglas and Sylvia a flat in London – I always thought that a lovely gesture on David's part - to which the senior Gilmours temporarily returned soon after our study concluded.

One of the impacts of my years in Ann Arbor was an enjoyment of college football, a virtual necessity for survival in the town. At first, I welcomed the emptying out of the town when the Wolverines were playing at Michigan Stadium. Saturday afternoons became a time when I could wander about the town with some ease, doing errands, having leisurely lunches, just walking about. But after a year or two the fate of the Wolverines became a pre-occupation. Those were the Bo Schembechler years and the teams were consistently excellent, with the buckeyes from Ohio State providing the only serious opposition. That rivalry was akin to Harvard – Yale but the quality of the football games was higher. Not that that was crucial, because Harvard–Yale had a snob appeal that Michigan - Ohio State could never have, not being Ivy.

One of the more interesting people I came to know a bit at Michigan was the dean, one William Hubbard. Bill had been the associate dean at NYU School of Medicine when I was there, and it was he who would call us in when our grades were poor and we were in some danger. It was Hubbard who admonished me about my Biochemistry grade in my first year at NYU, and made that crack about how I had done so well at Harvard in my major they expected me to perform as well in medical school. Hubbard had built up the Medical School in Ann Arbor during his tenure as Dean and was very well - regarded in Medical Education circles around the country.

Curiously, after four or five of my years at Michigan, Hubbard announced his intention to leave the school, not for another academic position, but instead to become Vice-President in charge of Medical Affairs at Upjohn, one of the biggest pharmaceutical companies in America, in the world in fact, a company based in Michigan. At that time such a shift from academic medicine to the world of the big drug companies was considered a betrayal of our academic community, where we struggled in relative anonymity for grants to move science forward millimeter by millimeter. Hubbard's act was deemed by those of us on the faculty to be an act of treason.

Several weeks after the announcement of his pending departure I met him at a reception in his honor at the Medical School. Because I knew him vaguely from his and my NYU days I felt free to ask him why he had taken the Upjohn job. He said, "Where else could I have 200 PhD's working for me on any problem of my choice?" Since Bill Hubbard was more an Administrator than a research scientist, I did not believe him then and do not believe him now. Nonetheless, I have come to see that Hubbard's move to the pharmaceutical industry at that time was but the beginning of a growing acceptance in medical academia of ties between faculty and private industry – not necessarily a "good thing" but it was a trend that would continue to the present time. And one which, as we shall see, influenced my years at Columbia.

My restlessness in Ann Arbor stemmed in some measure from the fact that I was at heart an Easterner. My Boston and New York roots tied me to the East Coast. It is true that the Boston and New York Symphony Orchestras were at that time far superior to the Detroit; the restaurants, including Japanese restaurants, in New York and Boston were much more respectable than in Ann Arbor; and most of my family and most of my friends lived on the East Coast. And so whenever I received a non-East Coast offer I was flattered but hesitant, as I really hankered for Tanglewood, the summer home of the Boston Symphony Orchestra, and the beaches of the North Shore of Boston, as well as the rapid pulse of East Coast life, especially of New York City life.

Since those days and my more or less constant wanderings around the world I have come to recognize the importance of feeling "right" about the place where one lives. Willa Cather pointed out, as have others, that when one is fortunate enough to find a place in which the heart finds a certain ease, a place in which one feels "at home," one ought never to leave. The opposite is surely true: One ought not to force oneself to live, except temporarily, in a place where one is less than perfectly at home. The Middle West was such a place for me, a fact I only came to understand over time. I was never comfortable there, despite a good, by any standards, job; an adequate if not lavish salary; and friends and colleagues who came to matter very much to me. It just did not work over-all for me there.

Thus, when the offer of a full professorship in Human Genetics and Pediatrics, with proper clinical responsibilities and copious laboratory space came from Columbia I was delighted and accepted with alacrity.

10

Escape to Columbia

Return to New York City

It is not an easy matter to move around, especially with family, from one country to the next, from one city to the next. But moving from Ann Arbor to New York was at least so much a no brainer for me that I rued the decision for not a single minute. I have often, as I have continued this pattern of movement over the years, asked myself if all the fuss and feathers of such relocations are worth the trouble and the answer to that is: it depends. When moving to a place where the heart may in fact find peace, a place in which one may presume to "belong", well then *ça vaut la peine,* as the French would say, it is worth the trouble. I have found that kind of comfort in but three or four places in the world in addition to Boston, my native place: New York City, Japan and Paris, the two marvelous cities and the country where I found the life style closest to my heart.

I have, of course, in the midst of my wanderings made mistakes. When the place has not been a fit, I have often struggled to make it one and usually failed: square peg in a round hole, sort of thing. Ann Arbor was one such failure.

I could never force myself successfully to be from the Midwest – it just did not suit me emotionally, despite the fact that it did offer me friends, colleagues, a satisfactory lifestyle; but it would never be what life could be, should be, and that is what a person owes himself – to be somewhere that fits him like a glove. Instead, I have all too often tried to adjust, sought out coffee shops and restaurants and activities that are satisfying without the town being precisely the right fit.

Later in life, my needs would be different as I came to be enamored both of the mountains and of the sea, but always the sea. There is of course a part of me that loves the mountains, the walks through the forest, the quickly flowing rivers, the clouds bending down to envelop the mountain tops. But, still, it is a struggle for me and not really *au fond* what or who I am. It is not just a question of a glimpse of one tree suffices for all – it is a question of where one is at peace, where the music suits a being.

Anyway, I moved to New York and it was, to say the least, eventful.

About two years before I moved back to The City, my dear friend Bob Krooth had accepted the chairmanship of the Department of Human Genetics and Development at the College of Physicians and Surgeons at Columbia University and he had moved to New York. He then urged me to join him in New York to help build the genetics group, with my special interest in clinical genetics being badly wanting at Columbia at that time. But there were two issues for Bob in New York: First, his own research suffered as he administered a growing Department; and, secondly, his relationship with Diana fell apart. And the two were related.

Bob and the group at Columbia had submitted a big Program Project Grant Renewal to the NIH, and Bob's section of the proposal did not fare well, and the funding of it was not recommended for renewal. Now, Bob was a very proud man in addition to being a superb scientist, and he took the critical remarks of the review committee very personally. He was embarrassed. We did not know at that time of his much earlier period of serious depression.

Diana went up to their Connecticut farm for the weekend following notification of the study section review, leaving Bob to his own devices. One of our faculty tried to rouse Bob in his apartment in New York on the Sunday, to no avail. So the concierge and our colleague Saul used a key to open the door. They found Bob in his study, brains blown out with a shotgun wound through the mouth.

The Connecticut State Police were dispatched to the farm to inform Diana of Bob's suicide. She was found at the farmhouse in the company of one of Bob's graduate students, for which none of us would ever forgive her, especially given Bob's evident NIH-induced pain at the time.

I was invited to give the Eulogy at the Columbia University Memorial Service for Bob, and that was a difficult thing to do. In my eulogy I culled the major elements of his life and discussed my views of his work, put something together which the faculty and staff reacted to very well, I daresay. He was brilliant and there was much to say. And from that time on – at least for a long while – I was regarded as a team player, someone to be counted on to put forward with verbal skill and good taste the party line. But I was devastated by Bob's suicide, found it hard to simply carry on as usual.

As I have thought about Bob's suicide over the years I believe it was because of it that I found it harder and harder to proceed in my professional life. I had started to see many patients with serious birth defects and potentially lethal diseases and would be mentally/emotionally a wreck on returning home to the suburbs to my ever-complaining, once-upon-a-time ingénue, whose primary concern came sadly to be the absence of a first-floor powder room in our Tudor house in Westchester County, a concern I could not find it in me to share.

I was also in a serious battle at Columbia with the chair of Obstetrics and Gynecology who did not at all buy into the idea - on the basis of which I was recruited to Columbia - that we would have a single clinical genetics unit across departmental lines, so the delivery of genetic services could be centralized under my direction but with all departments that wished to participating. That battle was worth fighting - as many in academia are not - since the clinical genetics Program could then apply for grant support which the smaller individual units could also do but with much less chance of success. The fight ended, after a few years of hard feelings, only with the death of said chairman of obstetrics from a heart attack. But by then the departmental lines had been drawn and there was little chance of cohesion.

So, I was fighting these issues at Columbia, growing my own research laboratory in environmental mutagenesis and establishing the clinical program while trying to hold off my feelings of sadness at the death of my dear friend and the at-home nagging of an implacable wife. One fine October day I was cooking hamburgers on the grill out back and the ingénue complained about the overcooking of the burgers, which inspired in me, after years of criticism from her about a range of personal things, the desire, the desperate desire, to be done with her. Despite my long-standing and heartfelt decision never to live apart from my children as I felt I had been left by my father when I was 13, I came to feel that my pain in staying was creating an untenable tension in the household, good neither for the children as they were growing up nor for me as I lived and worked. After I moved out, I tried to be very present in their lives - coaching their softball and baseball teams, spending every weekend with them in my three-bedroom New York City apartment, and having meals with them mid-week near their home– but the pain of our not living together during those years persists for them and me to this day.

The death of my friend and mentor, in the light of these other stresses, triggered in me an unexpected response. Brilliant as he was, and successful as he was in science, he had taken his life in some measure because of the harsh critique of his work by the NIH Study Section. He was shamed, and could not for whatever his reasons tolerate it. My tolerance of the fighting at home and at work gave out.

A second major blow came some few years later when Roy Schmickel was offered the Chairmanship of Human Genetics at the University of Pennsylvania: He was in his early 40's by then, and he and I had discussed the Penn offer before he took it. He left Ann Arbor a bit reluctantly but with enthusiasm. He was building the Department at Penn and he and his wife Leigh had just bought a house out on the Main Line. Soon thereafter he went up to Providence with his wife and kids for Thanksgiving with some friends and played squash the day after the Holiday. He crashed into a wall of the squash court, was unconscious for some days, and was paralyzed when he woke up. Turns out he had had an unknown-to-him congenitally narrow artery to his spinal cord which was severed when he hit the wall, leaving him unable to move arms or legs. He was now barely able to speak. He was eventually put on steroids to reduce the inflammation to his spinal cord and brain and, as steroids sometimes do, they ultimately resulted in a massive bleeding into his gastrointestinal tract which killed him.

I have lost many friends and colleagues along the way, but Roy's death – following close on the heels of Bob Krooth's suicide - gave me a special kind of pain. Roy, too, was a dear pal, and one does not have many such as one meanders through this life. He was a warm and friendly guy, we shared the same point of view about many of our colleagues at Michigan and elsewhere, and he was playful – a big, tall man who enjoyed life and a good laugh, even in the midst of our serious work. His wife Leigh stayed in Philadelphia for a while after his death and eventually moved with the kids and her new husband to Stone Mountain, Georgia, where we lost touch.

Despite these losses I kept working to build my Genetics Clinic and Laboratory programs. I found much pleasure in these, but beneath the surface I was not happy. I had moved into the City from the suburbs of Westchester, but went up each Wednesday evening for dinner out with the children and I attended both athletic and non-athletic events, going regularly to their schools and the playing fields of Scarsdale. I was especially focused on the academic lives of my children, as a measure of how they were getting along emotionally, and they were obviously thriving. They would go on to enroll in excellent colleges and they had many friends.

Being in the City, living the bachelor life, was a dream for every young man under a certain age. At my age, however, after an initial period of relief just to be on my own - feeding the children on "square plates", and burning a few hotdogs - and enjoying my newfound personal freedom, it became a tad tedious: the compulsory dates with various and sundry women, some lovely, smart, and exciting; some disturbingly dull and whiny. On balance it was a time in my life that I needed, having married at age 22 and never really having experienced life alone, in the City or anywhere.

I had experiences galore. There was the beautiful blond makeup artist for the PBS Channel in New York who smeared my face with gook as I prepared to appear on the McNeill-Lehrer Report to discuss my work at Three Mile Island. Yolanda was from the western part of Maryland, had come to New York four years earlier to practice cosmetology and had her own pad on the Upper East Side. It was a fourth-floor walkup, a tiny one bedroom which she shared with Charlie her Yorkshire terrier. Yolanda's bed was up on stilts, so we had to climb up there via a ladder to be able to embrace one another - over the violent objections of Charlie whose insane barking down below must have disturbed the whole building. It certainly made my sexual desires wane quickly. Still, I liked Yolanda, and we saw one another from time to time, mostly for "dinner and" ending up at my place on Morningside Heights.

I tried to see mostly women who were not in my field but inevitably I came to need more than Yolanda. I did have several "serious" relationships during that period, one in particular, but nothing which set both my heart and brain aflame.

After several years in New York I was invited to be Medical Director one summer for a 3-week Genetics Group tour of medical facilities in then still relatively closed China. In addition to being an enlightening medical journey to the land of the Barefoot Doctors and the land of highly developed herbal medicine, we were to visit the Forbidden City, rapidly growing Shanghai, and the charming city of Hangzhou. But, for all of that the journey to China was to be life-changing for me in another way.

I was advised well ahead of the tour by several participants that our Tour Guide was one Deborah Schwarz, a graduate student at both Harvard Law School and at the Russian Research Center. I was told that she was a superior guide, spoke Chinese after studying at Middlebury. We were to be in excellent hands. As Medical Director it seemed appropriate for me to meet her in advance of our departure and so she and I arranged a brief chat at the San Francisco International Airport, just prior to embarking for China.

The attraction was immediate, immutable and would be life-long. How does that sort of thing happen? I do not claim to know but there was never a doubt in my mind, or hers I suspect, that once embarked on our relationship we would simply be together – we married some six months after living together in the apartment I had rented on the Columbia Campus.

423

I suppose it was inevitable that where I lived would become a major focus of my life in New York City. As the moment of my departure from Westchester had approached – a moment of the most profound trauma - I began to look around for a pad in The City. I did not really want to live up at the Medical School area at 168th Street and Broadway. I preferred to try for a place closer to the Main Campus at 116th Street, where there would be more life, especially at night and on weekends, as well as greater proximity to Lincoln Center and Midtown, as well as the Village farther downtown.

The Columbia Housing Office on 119th Street was a centralized focus for University Housing of faculty and graduate students. I trundled over there a few weeks before Christmas, and was told that a Professor Karkas of Biochemistry was going back to his native Greece for a six - month sabbatical, taking his wife and daughter back with him, leaving their three – bedroom apartment empty between January and the following summer. The Housing Office urged me to meet with Karkas to see if we could work out an arrangement. With a fair amount of rapid give and take – my give, his take, it's the New York way when searching for an apartment - Professor Karkas and I came to terms and I moved in just after the New Year. He left his very modest furniture in place and it was a great blessing to me not to have to replace it. At least for the initial time I was to be there. So I became a resident at 423 West 120 Street, New York City, New York, 10032.

Becoming an apartment renter in The City is a major life's experience. When I was a medical student at NYU I had fended for myself in rooms in Manhattan, and later as part of a married couple in Brooklyn – but now I was a divorced professor, and the world was my oyster. The doorman at 423 was a marvelously warm and helpful guy named Sonny, who suggested that my first step might reasonably be to hire someone to "keep house." And he had just the person: one Mary Boone, an older lady from the 'hood whose work he knew well.

Mary was about five feet two inches tall, with a strong chin, a hairy upper lip, a mound of waggish hair piled on top of her head, thick glasses rarely removed from her face, and a waddle as opposed to a stride-like walk – Mary carried a bit too much weight for her height and she paid the price in a certain difficulty walking about.

Mary came by twice a week to keep me from being totally disheveled, new bachelor that I had become, and, more importantly, she rendered unto me her unambiguous opinions about the women I was seeing. She thus earned my deepest gratitude – largely, I daresay, because her judgment was almost always right. While Mary did not meet them all, she was never shy in expressing her opinion in regards to the ladies who passed through my apartment at 423 West 120th street.

The most telling perhaps was the serious involvement I

had with one of my lady friends whom Mary absolutely did not like. She tried, nonetheless, to keep her opinion somewhat to herself as I was becoming increasingly involved, Mary's views notwithstanding. But, while none of my egghead pals deigned to warn me off this very neurotic being, Mary knew little such hesitation and often conveyed to me in private her dislike for Paula's treatment of my kids, who visited on weekends and intermittently at other times. My kids shared Mary's view of Paula, which they had trouble enunciating given their tender years. Of course when I did hit the jackpot and began to bring my ultimate wife into the picture - someone to whom Mary gave her unqualified approval - I was reassured that Mary blessed the new deal and pressed on rapidly to make the relationship with Deborah a fait accompli.

I remember Mary's last New Year's Eve on this earth. I asked her where she was spending it, and she told me at her local bar over on 135th Street and Lenox Avenue, "You know the one," she said, " the one I have told you about before. The one with the blue lights flickerin' down."

Mary's age caught up with her and she finally died after we had "been together" some six years. The pastor from her Church, the A.M.E. Baptist Church not far from her tavern, called and asked if we could help the Congregation bury her properly. Several of us at 423 kicked in the necessary funds, and Deborah and I went up to the Church where she evidently had a lot of friends, as the Church was filled for the service. She would have been proud that we were there, as we, along with her sisters in the Church, were her family. I missed her then and miss her still.

I note here that while Mary's approval of my Ultimate Wife was not a pre-requisite stamp of approval Mary thought D was a "catch" and I felt the same way, so Mary's affection for D was confirmatory. D and I both had an affection for Mary Boone which we shared at the service for Mary at the A.M.E. Baptist Church - I knew Mary would have been pleased to see us together.

There were, of course, others in the building with whom I was involved: professors of note, brilliant and interactive colleagues in a diversity of Departments at the University. I was deeply pained at the death, during my second year at 423, of Joseph Bauke who lived in apartment 8G just down the hall from mine at 8E. Joe was head of the Department of Germanic Languages, was a German-born scholar of Goethe but with a wide range of tastes in opera and the arts. He had lived in the building some 28 years at the time I arrived. We talked from time to time *en passant*, but it was always a pleasure to hear what Joe was up to, as he was a cultured, Renaissance-type man who freely gadded about New York City during the academic year and spent his summers in Bavaria where his family had a house.

Perhaps one of the more interesting families on my floor was that of Russian brothers in their 30's, brought to the Mathematics Department at Columbia in year three of my seven-year stay at 423. There was a young American woman who lived with them, the wife of the older of the two professors. Since I spoke neither Russian nor Mathematics my only point of contact with the two brothers was via Veronica. The younger brother was in a wheelchair, having been afflicted with muscular dystrophy while still in Russia, and it was for treatment at the Neurological Institute at Columbia-Presbyterian Hospital that the two brothers had ostensibly come to the U.S.

But once here, their request, as brilliant Jewish emigres, for asylum was taken seriously and approved. The wheelchair-bound brother Dmitri had developed a unique mathematical proof of an old theorem that no one had ever been able to come up with. He was widely recognized as a genius in mathematics, a world-class addition to the faculty. Dmitri was given a MacArthur Grant of some $500,000 and was a celebrity, finally secure and able to support the family.

And then there was the bane of my existence at 423, one John Taylor, who lived directly above me on the ninth floor. John was the son of the main American prosecutor of the Nazis at Nuremberg, also John Taylor; but this younger John Taylor was a druggie who played hard rock at all hours of the night and day, mostly at night. Drove me crazy. I banged on the ceiling of my apartment which was his floor, I banged resolutely on the pipes that ran between our floors, and I called him on the phone, plaintively at first, more forcefully as time went on. Finally, I found The Way: I threatened and finally did call in the local police and John did not like that at all, given all the dope he must have had in his apartment. With the advent of the Men in Blue John lined his apartment with sound-resistant tiling and my life changed for the better, though there was never any love lost between us.

• • •

Of note re John Taylor:

I became interested, once the acrimony dimmed a bit, how it was that John lived in the building. His father was the story. Telford Taylor was born in Schenectady, went to Williams and then Harvard Law School, entering into Government work in Washington in the 1930's. Major Taylor worked with Robert Jackson in military intelligence in the 1940's. Jackson was ultimately to become lead Prosecutor at Nuremberg in 1945, and when he left in 1946, Lt Col, then Brigadier General, Taylor was assigned to take his place, becoming Prosecutor of many of the Nazis – both military men and industrialists - in the mid-40's. General Taylor made his way soon thereafter to New York, becoming a Professor at Columbia University Law School, where he taught for many years. His wife, John Taylor's mother, died in the mid-60's. Professor Taylor eventually added a professorship at Yeshiva University's Benjamin Cardozo School of Law, while living still at Morningside Heights. General Taylor was active in pro-Israel causes, wrote extensively about McCarthyism, which he hated, and the Vietnam War, of which he was also highly critical. My assumption is that the younger John held onto his apartment at Columbia by dint of his father's connections to Columbia as well as the General's distinguished reputation in legal circles in New York and around the world.

• • •

At work I tried to keep my focus on developing the Clinical Genetics Program at Columbia, as described above, and over the years had mixed success at that. The inter-departmental wars were, as is often the case in academia, an impediment to progress and certainly to a happy enjoyment of what success we did have. These wars were over primacy in the field - who was to be the public face of the Program, what space was to be used in which Department, etc. I started a more regional program involving the many geneticists we had in the New York Area, under sponsorship of the March of Dimes Birth Defects Foundation. That was great fun, meeting with colleagues every few weeks, helping to expand the delivery of clinical genetic services in Greater New York and throughout the State.

This activity led indirectly to one of my grand adventures when I was at Columbia. I received a call one day from Washington, the Pan American Health Organization (PAHO, as it is commonly called). I hopped a plane to Washington to discuss in person a genetical problem in the Caribbean Islands, specifically on Grand Cayman Island. Seems the Island had three or four "population centers" but until recent times each area was relatively separated from the others. That in turn had led to inbreeding, with the cousins, for example, from the East End reproducing with their cousins from the East End, the people from the West Bay marrying and reproducing with their relatives of West End origin. PAHO had received reports that there were many babies on Grand Cayman who were afflicted with congenital abnormalities, congenital but not always lethal. Thus there was a population of persons waiting to be examined and studied. PAHO asked me to go to Grand Cayman and do some preliminary work to determine the nature of the diseases being seen.

I began a review of the history of the *Cayamanas* which was fascinating from both a genetical point of view and a humanistic point of view, and I booked a flight to Georgetown, its capital, via Miami on Cayman Airways. I met with Island officials primarily in the Public Health sector, including in particular Mr Linford Pearson, the Secretary to the Minister for Health who had the portfolio. Mr Pearson – now Dr Pearson - was very helpful in our organizing the project by assigning the country's lone Public Health Nurse, one Josie Solomon of the East End, to work more or less full-time with me, and later with my team from Columbia. Ms Solomon was a fountain of information, some of it written down, some of it, perhaps most of it, simply in her head.

First to be dealt with were the Wolfmen of West Bay, people who walked around on all fours. Next, there was the probably metabolic disease also of West Bay which resulted in severe mental retardation and characteristic bushy eyebrows and odd facies, with death in early childhood. Then, there was the strikingly high rate of congenital deafness among East Enders, perhaps the highest rate of genetic high tone hearing loss in any human population. And Lord knows what else we were going to find.

The history of the Island revealed it to be then and nowadays a major tourist attraction in the Caribbean, very high tech and highly developed, with excellent roads between districts, gorgeous sandy beaches and a very active deep sea diving industry. Lurking in the background, of course, was the banking industry, a center for offshore concealment of large sums of money for its clients – an industry that would not welcome sensationalism or anything negative about the country, like "men and women walking on all fours."

We nonetheless needed a systematic approach. With several genetic colleagues well-versed in doing family pedigrees, we set about doing detailed family histories on all the patients that Nurse Solomon and others would introduce us to in the Towns of West Bay, Georgetown, the East End and the North Side on the Island. After months of detailed work we emerged with huge pedigrees of Caymanians of all ages, going back many years, often three to six generations. The interviews with old timers - people in their 80's and even 90's - were especially revealing of detailed family stories, stories which younger Caymanians in their 30's and 40's were unable to tell us. That was like the senior member of the Maple Syrup Urine Disease family I had studied in Plymouth, North Carolina, during my medical school days. The treasure trove of information about these families with suspected genetic disorders was to come from a very few progenitors who really knew the Islanders in their districts.

Step by step we analyzed these pedigrees and did physical examinations on patients who had been identified as possibly affected with one or more of the suspect genetic disorders. In the end we had firm evidence of the strongly Mendelian inheritance of congenital deafness, with cases largely confined to the East End. We documented the recessive patterns of inheritance in the populous West Bay area of what we called Cayman Disease, a kind of brain disorder that affected balance and intellect and resulted in the Wolf Man Syndrome, with affecteds walking on all fours in the West Bay - they almost never left their homes except after dark. And, also in the West Bay area we found a recognized metabolic disorder referred to as San Fillipo Syndrome, a lethal form of retardation that was caused by abnormal buildup of a complex sugar – a mucopolysaccharide – which these children could not metabolize.

I got into trouble with this work in two ways. First, Columbia was not enchanted with my spending months at a time in the Caribbean. Who could blame them, except the work was, I felt, both important and interesting. I loved the work itself and was determined to do it. Our work eventually resulted in the building of a school for the people who walked on all fours, and the provision of resources for the care and education of the population that needed physical therapy and special education. It was for me and my colleagues very satisfying, indeed.

The larger issue developed with the Pan American Health Organization (PAHO) itself, the ultimate sponsors of our efforts. The local Caymanian newspaper and radio station focused their reporting on me and my team from New York, but especially on me. I always cited that I was a Columbia professor and a representative of PAHO, the international health group responsible under the World Health Organization for medical care in the Caribbean. But, both the Caymanian Government and the public identified the program heavily with me personally, and the PAHO people resented my new-found notoriety on the Islands. I sensed this and made every effort to attribute funding and organization to the PAHO group in Washington and Jamaica, its headquarters in the Caribbean.

The medical community on Grand Cayman, and the

Minister for Health and his Cabinet Secretary, all were delighted with the Genetics Program and they, too, identified the Program with me - perfectly reasonable as I was the only geneticist on the Island and the duly appointed delegate from PAHO.

Eventually after about three years of effort, documenting what was and what needed to be done to both treat the patients and prevent many more cases, with a palpable resistance growing at Columbia to my annual two to three month-long absences, I had to take a step back and help the Program link up to the nearer-by University of Miami, which made a certain sense.

My deep-seated pleasure in being of use to the patients and to the Island far exceeded the discomfort induced by the sparring that went on at Columbia and at PAHO. Further, I was emotionally moving away from these kinds of internal and external battles over primacy and recognition. I wanted, needed, less and less of that.

And when my request of the NIH for funding for the program to be siphoned through Columbia so the University would get its share of overhead and direct costs, when that research request was rejected, I had no basis from Columbia's point of view for continued long absences.

But, in fact, the rejection itself was complex. We had been site visited by an NIH team and each of our projects was assessed separately as well as part of the whole. One of the NIH site visitors, in the course of critiquing one of the biochemical neurology projects, brutalized, absolutely brutalized one of my young co-investigators - a particularly promising, brilliant young neurologist. No need to embarrass him en route to declining to support the project, but some of my co-scientists knew, probably know, no limits on their intellectual and personal clout when in positions of power over others. Human nature, I suppose, but not on my watch.

At about this time I had organized a small commercial diagnostic genetics laboratory called Diagen over in Teaneck, New Jersey. I arranged for venture capital funding and assumed the position of part-time medical director of the lab. Now, according to the by-laws at Columbia that regulated faculty participation in such related but outside activities, each full-time faculty member was entitled to spend 20 percent of his or her time in non-University-related professional functions. A professor at the Law School, for example, would often earn outside monies by working a day a week at one of New York's prestigious firms, and many did. It was a time during which, for better or worse, ties between medical faculty and commercial interests around the country were growing.

The Dean at the College of Physicians and Surgeons at Columbia called me in, and I went along to his office, accompanied by the businessmen owners of Diagen. The University's position, in writing, was that insofar as I was on the faculty and insofar as the lab had been built around me the University was entitled to 50 percent ownership of what we had created. The owners – I was a very minor shareholder – refused, as did I, believing that was pure greed on the part of the University. Needless to say that was the beginning of a "difficult" period in my formal ties to the school. The laboratory went on to do very well, as genetic testing was growing. Diagen was ultimately sold to a larger enterprise, by which time I was long gone.

Meanwhile, however, I continued to fulfill my research, teaching and clinical duties at Columbia as usual.

Mohammed Hafez was an Egyptian physician who served a large population in the city of Mansoura, Egypt, about 30 minutes from Alexandria on the Mediteranean. Dr Hafez had come to the United States under the auspices of our National Academy of Medicine in Washington. I was never sure how this practicing pediatrician who lived up-stream on the Nile had come to visit the U.S. for six months, but the National Academy called Dr. Paul Marks, Vice President for Health Sciences at Columbia , one day and asked if Mohammed could come for a couple of months to Columbia to see how we handled patients with birth defects and heritable diseases. Paul, in turn, called me and asked me to take Mohammed Hafez on. He said that Mohammed was interested in both my lab work in cytogenetics, and in our clinical genetics program. I agreed and Dr. Hafez of Egypt showed up a few weeks later.

From the first time we met, I liked Mohammed. He was a soft-spoken physician, who worked, he reported, in a very busy pediatric center at Mansoura University, north of Cairo. He had several younger colleagues, he told me, but they were untrained in genetical problems and focused their energies on infectious diseases and malnutrition - the then major problems in the pediatric population in Egypt. Patients with congenital anomalies and inherited diseases, fewer in number, were thus somewhat neglected and Mohammed wanted to be of service to those patients. He faithfully attended our weekly genetics conferences, spent time in my laboratory learning the techniques of chromosome preparation and analysis in order to diagnose at least some of the congenital malformation children. Further, Mohamed was much liked by all of our staff.

From the outset, it was clear that one of Mohammed's main goals was to get me to come to Egypt for a professional visit. After he returned to Egypt he was as good as his word: he paid for a ticket for me on Egypt Air so I could visit him in Cairo and especially at Mansoura University at his clinic. I hemmed and hawed, a bit anxious because I was unsure how welcome a Jew would be at that difficult time in Egypt and the Middle East. I planned an itinerary which took me from New York to Cairo, thence to Israel via Athens, a routing which enabled Israel not to be recorded on my passport – a serious no-no for a Jew travelling in the Middle East to Muslim countries at that time.

Cairo itself was a maddening, manic place but so fascinating with its bazaars and array of little shops with proprietors on the streets trying to sell their wares. I stayed at Giza out by the pyramids at the distinguished Mena House, and Mohammed introduced me to his colleagues in Cairo and showed me around. Of particular note was the seniormost human geneticist in Egypt at the time, one Dr. Nemat Hashem, a sophisticated, very knowledgeable Professor of Pediatrics and Chief of the Medical Genetics Center at Ain Shams Univerity in Cairo, perhaps Cairo's best medical university. Professor Hashem's English was excellent and while I had met her briefly once at an annual meeting of the

American Society of Human Genetics of which she was an international member, I had never spent serious time chatting with her. She served as consultant to Dr. Hafez and saw some of his more diagnostically complex cases. Nemat Hashem had me visit her at Ain Shams where she showed me her impressive Genetics Center. She also helped me buy a few items at the Cairo Bazarre – she was a superb bargainer.

After my visit in Cairo, Mohamed had a car and driver take me to Mansoura where he and his wife had moved from their apartment for the duration of my stay, so I would be comfortable, there being no hotel of quality at that time in the city. We had a dinner with Mohamed's colleagues at a local restaurant. I enjoyed the colleagues but the stuffed grape leaves filled with delicious meats AND squirming little worm-like beasties were not at all appealing though I had to make the effort.

There followed three days of intense patient care: the families brought their wee ones from everywhere, seemingly, wrapped often in rags and covered with flies, looking for diagnostic and therapeutic help. The long lines from the clinic doors out onto the street ran a solid city block and I was busy from eight in the morning until six or seven at night, just about non-stop. I was depressed and exhausted after those days but I did not want to let Mohammed down, or his able staffers who assisted me. Above all I felt obliged to see the patients who had waited months to consult the famous pediatrician from New York. But when the diarrhea hit me I began weakening, and had to tell Mohamed I needed a break.

On the evening of the third day in Mansoura I was to

give a lecture to the Red Crescent Society of Mansoura and Alexandria. The Red Crescent Society was, of course, related to the International Red Cross - originally, it was part of the International Federation of Red Cross and Red Crescent Societies (IFRC); but being Muslim and Arab countries - in this instance Egypt - numerous countries refused to be represented by a cross and chose the crescent instead. Mohamed advised me not to let on that I was going from Egypt to Israel, i.e., not to let on that I was Jewish. That suggestion alarmed me but I intended to give the talk anyway. I note that at that time the Red Crescent Society of Egypt, as other Red Crescent Societies in the Middle East, was becoming increasingly influenced by the Muslim Brotherhood more than the politically neutral Red Cross. I did what Mohamed asked but was tense throughout my lecture which was simply about our work in experimental and clinical genetics.

On the morning of the fifth day in Mansoura, at a time when my physical exhaustion was increasing and my emotional commitment to continue to see patients was ebbing, I told Mohamed that I wanted to visit Luxor and the Valley of the Kings, and the next day we were off.

We rode the overnight train from Cairo to Luxor, a train I dubbed the Magyar Express because the train itself was made in Hungary, the tracks in Egypt; but the tracks were a tad too narrow so the train shook back and forth all night long. The bathrooms on the train had terrible plumbing and so the floors of the men's room were covered in one to two inches of urine, rendering a late night pee impossible. Plus there was a uriniferous odor, how could there not be, permeating the train, making the trip a veritable 12-hour misery.

But, Luxor was worth the misery. I had seen the Antiquities Museum in Cairo, with the Black Cat of Bastet made of Bronze, and the heavily jeweled King Tut Exhibit at the Metropolitan Museum in New York. All such things Egyptian intrigued me. In those exhibits the beauty of the carvings and stones was overwhelming. Here in Luxor, I knew, there would be mostly empty tombs since thieves - tomb raiders - had long ago relieved the tombs of their relics. Still, the sarcophagi, pots, and maybe a few mummies would be exciting to see. And just to be where Tuthankhamun and Ramses had been entombed , well, the thrill of a lifetime, really.

We waited in the lobby of one of the old hotels in Luxor from six a.m. when we arrived, until nine a.m. when the tombs opened for visits, and I nodded off briefly. The hotel was fully booked so we could not get a room, the lobby it had to be. But my sense of excitement about the Howard Carter discoveries knew no bounds and I was anxious to proceed into the tombs. Just to walk in those vaults made me think of an age long, long ago when such tombs were built, such kings and queens so honored. I thought of the supposed curses that the Carter people suffered as a result of having invaded these holy places, but I also rhapsodized about the sense of excitement they must have felt with the discovery of each tomb, in the earlier part of the 20th century.

One of the most impressive sites in Luxor, ancient Thebes, was the massive Karnak Temple, which was in its time - 2000 B.C. - the largest ancient religious site in the world. I knew little about Karnak and so this was all an education. The mix of temples and pylons admitted the visitor to the

Middle and New Kingdoms of ancient Egypt, and only some of Karnak was open to the public so there is much more I could not see. But the power of the over- whelmingly large stone pillars was awe-inspiring, built as it was to honor the many gods of Egypt's ancient world.

We did not stay the night in Luxor, but went back to Cairo, spent the night at the Mena House and were off the next day to Israel via Athens. Much genetics in Israel, where the frequency of disease genes among the heterogeneous populations of Israel was under close scrutiny. Mohamed and I kept in touch for a few years, finally lost touch. I tried from Paris later on to make contact to no avail. I was sad finally to learn that he had died of stomach cancer about 15 years after our time in Mansoura and Luxor, a good man.

The Decision

To leave Columbia was not especially difficult: I had been separating for a number of years. I was simply tired of the academic world. Maybe bored, but in any event not interested any longer in grant writing, in running a lab or a clinic even, and certainly I was uninterested in the administrative goings-on in my departments at the College of Physicians and Surgeons.

Along the way I had been taking courses in fiction and nonfiction writing on the main campus on Morningside Heights. And when it came time for my Sabbatical, I had a choice, as I saw it, between spending six months doing, learning, molecular biology - the clear wave of the future in genetics - and staying close to 423 and taking more writing courses. I opted without hesitation for the writing classes.

The best one was at Skidmore College in Saratoga Springs that summer. Offered by the New York State Writers' Institute of Albany, under the guidance of Frank McCourt whose work on his Irish roots I loved. The class kept me writing fiction full-time for a solid six weeks and I liked it enormously. It was not that what I produced was so good, I was still in the formative stages after all.

It was, rather, that I was just happy doing the writing. I could sit in silence, typing out my ideas for stories and the stories themselves: it was the peace of it that captured me - and as time wore on I was getting better at it, I could tell. But I was in it for the tranquility and sheer enjoyment the process gave me. I was not thinking of embarking on a writing career, making my living being a writer, joining literary societies and interacting with those who lived by the pen, sort a speak. I had had my fill of weekly staff meetings, professional gatherings, annual meetings, eager students, that stuff was no longer satisfying – this new direction would be introspective, for better or worse, while the genetics was for me a career in the fullest sense. I had success at it, if judged by my professorship, my grants, my elected and appointed positions, my colleagues' admiration. But for whatever the reasons, I had finished what I set out to do after Boston Latin, after Harvard, and after Medical School, by becoming a professor.

When it came to the end of my sabbatical I elected to spend two years on a formal leave, did what I could to see to my academic duties including my students and those who worked with me in the Genetics Clinic and in my Laboratory; resigned from Columbia and moved with my Ultimate Wife to the Berkshires in Western Massachusetts/Eastern New York State.

I discussed my departure with Deborah, who was by then not only my wife but increasingly my soulmate. My movement towards her over those years was in fact a movement toward the better parts of my being. And towards my writing self. When she accompanied me a few years earlier to our first Columbia dinner dance, at Low Library, attired in a feathery wrap, she looked sensational and was a whiff of fresh air in that staid atmosphere. We shared a love of the arts and she supported my impulse toward the freer world of the imagination. With her all things, my giving up the professorship at Columbia included, were possible.

I should add that I knew full well that most of my genetics colleagues would not understand my decision to cut myself free. And I have learned that floating unattached, with no secure base, is perhaps one of life's most difficult passages. But, I had done it voluntarily - I was sure of my instincts and wavered not much. I did what I could to ensure a semblance of an income, informed Columbia of my decision, and headed with Deborah to the Berkshires.

11

The Berkshire Years/ Environmental Health

Austerlitz, New York, and Pittsfield, Massachusetts

As I walked in the garden of our 40 acre spread in the Berkshire Hills, the fall air was crisp. I held my ten-month-old son Noah tightly with only his face exposed. We were in mid- October, the foliage had turned into a multi-colored rainbow, the grass was cut, for the season, I hoped, and I was very happy about our new life. I raised our son Noah up to show him the starry night, and he said, "Moon" - his first word beyond Dada and Mama.

I had signed on at the major medical center in the region, the Berkshire Medical Center, where I had set up a new genetics service so I could earn a buck or two, a unit that was for this country-side medical facility a unit of great pride, very modern and au courant as genetics was in the practice of medicine. The professor from Columbia brought a bit of notoriety to the institution, as well as some resentment from medical practitioners. Over-all, I was pleased to participate in the strengthening of the reputation of the Berkshire Medical Center as a Center of Excellence.

But I was not really there for that. I had long wanted to extend my laboratory research on in vitro mutagens and carcinogens to real life environmental health issues of the day. I went to Washington to court the support of our local Congressman, Silvio Conte, who had risen to become chair of the powerful House Appropriations committee. Silvio Conte was a consummate politician and he looked out for the best interests of his Berkshire County constituency. He asked what could he do to further our work which at that time had initiated a series of a highly scientific think-tank like studies on environmental mutagens, mechanisms of damage to DNA, the effect of oxidative stress, etc. I had assembled a group of about a dozen scientists from the U.S. and Europe, and we met regularly to discuss the environmental health issues of the day. We needed, however, to have core funding to establish our Environmental Health Institute as a permanent player in the field. That funding was what I would attempt to extract from the Congressman.

It should be noted that I had served for some years on the Board of Scientific Counselors of the National Institute of Environmental Health Sciences, which Board oversaw the scientific content of the research done both at the NIEHS in the Research Triangle Park, North Carolina, as well as the research done across the country via grants and contracts awarded to university-based investigators. Further, I was being actively considered for the position of Director of the NIEHS, a position I would have had to accept if offered.

However, there was at that time no black Director of any of the then eight National Institutes of Health - a gross error in judgment somewhere along the line. That had to be corrected, and it was and I understood the need, no regrets here.

I have often wondered what my life would have been like had I become Director of NIEHS. We would have had to move to North Carolina; I would have become a serious administrator of science and its operatives - it would have been a different life, not necessarily a better life, just different. I would certainly not have been able to continue my writing efforts, for whatever they were worth, which was a lot to me, not much important to the world.

On balance, I remained free(r) and continued to do what I liked, in my own way. I surrounded myself with a small group of colleagues whose interests in environmental medicine I shared; and we proposed to do studies in depth to bring hard-nosed assessments of data and findings on environmental health to the scientific world. I laid all this out to Rep. Conte and he wanted to support my idea. He as I wanted to bring a group of distinguished biomedical scientists (and jobs) to his Berkshires. He was able to do so with annual grants to us in the amount of about $500,000 a year for five years. He was a gracious man and we owed him a lot. We had our meetings in Berkshire County and nearby and the public was well aware of Rep. Conte's interest in these matters. I offered to name our Environmental Health Institute in his honor. He agreed and so we grew the Silvio O. Conte Institute for Environmental Health in Pittsfield Massachusetts, writing and publishing a series of studies on the environmental health effects of chemicals and on the mechanisms by which such agents do their damage. Rep. Conte died of prostatic cancer some years later and that was for me and the Institute and the country a great loss. A major part of my post-Columbia education derived from my many trips to Washington to The House and to his office to discuss the status of our work with the Congressman so he could defend the annual appropriation before his colleagues on the Appropriations Committee.

In addition to being a period of personal change and continued scientific activity, the time in Western Massachusetts was life-affirming. I had, after all, left Columbia and survived. Maybe even thrived. I was writing stories, had somehow found a balance between my medical science and the writing life. But the world around us was changing and I felt the need to expand the nature of the studies we were doing, from the interesting but somewhat dry science to more applied environmental health work. I had, after all, been involved with the radiation-exposed populations of Hiroshima and Nagasaki; the chemically-exposed population of the Love Canal in Upstate New York; and the radiation-exposed of Three Mile island in Pennsylvania. And that was environmental health research which was particularly important to the populations at risk.

During the late '80's and early '90's, the Berlin Wall was beginning to crumble. President Reagan had seen to that, and the world would, it appeared, be treated to the sight of unparalleled massive environmental contamination of a large region, Eastern Europe. I promptly sought and obtained funding to go on what I called a Marco Polo-style trip, to try to assess in a preliminary way the health effects of the chemical and radiation contamination which the Soviets had effectively kept secret.

I flew to Paris and thence to Prague, Bratislava, Budapest, Kiev, Moscow, and to the World Health Organization in Geneva to try to make sense of the environmental work that needed done. I spoke mainly with fellow scientists, but also with governmental people in a position to know what we might expect. It became clear that extensive research would be needed to document the effects on the populations exposed to pesticides used in farming, on chemical plant workers, on uranium miners, et alia. But it was also clear as I wandered that the scientific establishment in the involved countries - The Ukraine, Soviet Russia, the Czech Republic, Hungary - was minimally prepared to conduct such studies. The world of science had moved smartly on methodologically in the West during the Cold War, but not in the East. Equipment was outdated, current books on biomedicine were in short supply, and the scientists themselves were woefully underpaid and ill-trained. So, what to do?

I organized a Symposium in Prague, and we held several days of talks with researchers from many of the involved countries. Out of these discussions evolved a newer version of the Conte Environmental Health Institute which morphed into the Comité International sur L'Environnement et La Santé.

The time in the Berkshires was a semi-pastoral period between Columbia and New York City on the one hand, and Paris on the other. Our Environmental Health Institute produced a series of Monographs on Genetic Risk

Assessment, Oxidative Stress, Approaches to Exposed Human Populations, and other, I think useful reviews on the state of environmental health research of the time.

And on a personal level it gave Deborah and myself a child we wanted to educate in the best possible way, not just in the traditions of rural Massachusetts and New York State where we lived, but also we wanted him to be an educated man with a global orientation to life.

Further, I wanted to spend a period of my advancing years in Europe, especially in France. Thus the formation of our Comité International represented to me an opportunity to move the center of my research efforts and life to Paris, to build a life there which I had long dreamed of living.

Convinced of the need for the studies on the health effects in Eastern Europe, I convinced my wife and Mother – who by then had moved from Boston to live with us, especially with her new grandson – we packed up Noah and darling little bichon frise Genevieve de Saint Bart and we all boarded an Air France flight from Newark to Charles de Gaulle in Paris. It was January 1, 1993; the snow was falling, the plane was being de-iced and we were ready, all of us, for a great adventure.

All was going well, until just after the dinner on board, when Mother, who by that time in her life had been diagnosed with Parkinson's, could not find her teeth. We searched all around our seating area, to no avail and Mother was in an absolute panic. The steward and stewardesses then had to initiate a search of the dinner trays, which were not stacked up in any particular order. The search of the randomly stacked trays finally netted Mother's teeth much to everyone's relief.

One of the members of our study sessions at the Conte had been a professor of Mathematics at the University of Texas, and when he heard of the impending move to Paris, he suggested that I contact the secretary of an international mathematics group, which was based in France, regarding housing. Therese Bricheteau told me she herself lived with her mother in an 80 square meter apartment in the fashionable 16th arrondissement. Therese's mother was ailing and Therese wished to give up her job and move with her mother to their second home in the countryside, in southwest France. She offered to try to have her apartment transferred to me if the building's owners – a society of miners who had extensive real estate holdings in Paris – were willing.

I flew to Paris, saw the apartment with Mme Bricheteau, and went with her to the owner's offices on the Champs Élysées, and I signed a lease. It was by no means as easy as that sounds since the reality required months of negotiations by mail, and a return trip to Paris – hard times everywhere! – before we could take possession. But, we persisted and finally on that snowy day in early 1993 we flew to Paris to stay.

12

Paris, *Enfin:* Becoming a Writer

The Great Adventure that became Paris began with a sense of excitement and also uncertainty. We knew we were headed to 33, avenue du General Sarrail to live. The 16th arrondissement was known to be an almost suburban, pleasant part of Paris, one which had been a separate rural town until the early 20th century. The living was thus likely to be fine, and it was, with excellent patisseries, cafes, bistros, and, a boon, Parc des Princes, the stadium where the Paris Saint Germain Soccer Club played, plus the Roland Garros Tennis Club at which the French Open was held each May.

But the work that awaited me was very uncertain. Could I build this program in which a group of internationally recognized scientists studied the effects of the environmentally-contaminated countries of Eastern Europe? How to do it? Where to base it? How to fund it?

I had ideas on all of these. The Hôpital Saint Louis in the 10th arrondissement was a major center for cancer research, just as it had been for leprosy treatment back in the 16th and 17th centuries. The Board of the Hôpital was interested,

I was told by genetic colleagues in Paris, in the environmental genetic studies we were proposing to do. I made contact with the powers that were, and submitted a written proposal that outlined the planned work of our Comité International sur L'Environnement et La Santé. The review group at the Hôpital St Louis endorsed the program, invited us to become a part - albeit a separate part - of the Hospital and I was honored that we were accepted by its scientific review committee.

The Hôpital Saint Louis was at least 400 years old. It had been founded by Henri IV at the time of one of the great Plagues of the early 17th century, and was named for Henri's grandfather Louis IX, who had died of dysentery in Tunisia. Under Henri the plague patients of Paris were isolated at the facility on the hill over-looking Paris, and the Hôpital became, in the years after the plague epidemics, a center for Leprosy and thus Dermatology, and later Hematology, especially cancers of the bloodstream.

I shall always remember the location of the Hospital, close-by the Canal Martin on Avenue Claude Vellefaux, in the Tenth, where I would often walk and sit at lunchtime as the locks of the narrow Canal were raised and lowered to allow small craft to pass. Thus it was an idyllic sort of place with a distinguished medical history.

It also had a magnificent garden and courtyard just outside the original buildings of the Hospital, a peaceful place for patients to go and enjoy the old trees and flowers. It was in one of those original buildings the Administrators of the Hospital proposed to have our group situated.

At my first meeting with the Administration of the

Hôpital Saint Louis I expected to be welcomed to the Hôpital and to have the terms of our entry and lease explained. The Administrators explained that the Hospital was in the midst of a building campaign, an effort was being made to bring the ancient buildings up to date with modern wiring, plumbing per the construction codes of the day, and proper heating and decorating. Cost to the Comité: 25,000 French francs for the privilege of occupying a two - room suite of offices in the old part of the Hôpital.

I was taken aback because we were in the business of trying to raise money for our research projects in far-away countries, and there were no 25,000 francs sitting idly anywhere. Further, the Hôpital Saint Louis was a municipal hospital and I begrudged the City of Paris my indebtedness to it. But, after discussions with the members of the Comité and facing the evident fact that none of my colleagues had the requisite sum available in their research coffers, I received permission to borrow the money personally, signed the papers of agreement and soon thereafter moved into a very old building with windows on the garden, but no elevator, no fresh paint, and no up-to-date wiring as yet. The view on the garden was, however, a very great pleasure to behold.

One of my primary colleagues through all of these negotiations and beyond was a molecular geneticist, one of the stars of the hospital's staff, Christian Larsen. Christian was a prolific author and he asked me to check out the English of his scientific papers from time to time, though he was really fluent – his papers needed minimal fine tuning, language-wise. I would often stop by his office and we would have long talks about the Hôpital, the world of politics (lots of politics, American and French), our families, and he confided in me the story of his father.

His dad had been a pharmacist and he was a member of the French Resistance. He was imprisoned by the Nazis during the Occupation of France when Christian was a very young boy. Much to everyone's relief he appeared in 1945 after a long, horrendous absence in the camps. But he was afflicted with tuberculosis and died eight months after his return. Christian and I discussed the trauma of his father's death - disappearance, reappearance, disappearance - particularly in relation to my own father's disappearance from my life when I was but 13, in 1948. But the trauma of the War and Christian's father's dying a kind of hero, was not comparable. I respected the manner in which Christian carried on and built a life of quality and accomplishment despite his dad's death.

He was my one true friend at the Hôpital and our talks sustained me in that period of adjustment to life in difficult-to-live-in Paris - wonderful Paris, beautiful Paris, but not easy to live in Paris. The rules and regulations had to be mastered, and above all the people had to be, well, adjusted to.

The gardienne Mme Devray at 33, avenue du General Sarrail was one example of the kind of person to whom we had to adjust. We had to rely on Monsieur and Madame to help us get settled in at 33, as they held the keys to the mail box, the storage locker, could tell us where to place our garbage, and knew who to call for hooking up the gas and electricity. I had in fact come to Paris several months in advance of our move-in date to try to arrange all these things including, importantly, to open a bank account. It was all an adventure.

I flew to Paris some four months before we were to move in that January day of our family's arrival in Paris. I planned to open a bank account in the neighborhood, have the gas and electricity hooked up, and organize the internet and telephone service so all would be ready for the family. I had been warned that to initiate the services in the apartment with Gaz de France, France Télécom, etc, I would need evidence of a bank account so as to be able to leave the service providers with a means of automatic deduction from our account.

I got a cashier's check for $10,000 U.S. (good as cash, I was promised) from my bank in New York, the Key Bank, and cheerfully presented myself, passport and check in hand in Paris. Five consecutive French banks refused to open the account. While we had signed the lease on 33, avenue du General Sarrail, and I had a Xerox copy of the lease with our names and our address duly inscribed, the Société des Mines, which owned the building, had not yet returned a signed copy to us as proof of occupancy. Further, the banks argued, I had no paid bill from France Telecom, EDF (Électricité de France), GDF (Gaz de France) or any other utility so how did they know we were residing in France?

My argument that the dollar Bank Check was "good as cash" fell on deaf ears at Crédit Lyonnais, La Banque Postale, Crédit Agricole, Société Générale, and BNP Paribas. I returned home to the States, tail between my legs, embarrassed at having failed in this seemingly simplest of chores: opening a bank account, even with the money in hand.

My friend Christian Larsen at the Hôpital Saint Louis later would regale me with stories of how when he had gone to the U.S. in 1986 to do research for two years at Yale as a Research Fellow, he handed over $10.00 - ten dollars - to the First National Bank and Trust of New Haven and walked out within twenty minutes with both Savings and Checking accounts, including a book of blank checks for his use. I obviously had much to learn about the French system of banking, billpaying, etc. – Paris is not New Haven.

The Devrays had come to Paris many years earlier from Lille up north. M. Devray, M. Louis Devray, was a personable gentleman, maybe in his later 50's, who was, when we first met him, some months post-head and neck surgery for a spreading cancer of the mouth. His jaw had been partially removed and he had a tracheostomy, so speaking was not easy for him. But, he was obviously a kind man, easy to relate to despite his disability and discomfort. His duties were to see to the waste management at 33, avenue du General Sarrail

Mme Devray, on the other hand, was the proverbial French gardienne: nasty to a fault, protective, she claimed, of the national identity of La France against the inroads in "her" building of the few but not to be trusted foreigners – "Etrangers"- from les Etats – Unis, le Portugal, L'Angleterre et al. Need the basement storage area that comes with your lease? Good luck extracting the key from Mme Devray who has loaned out the storage area to others. Maybe six months from then? Need a place to store your bicycle? Should have thought of that before you brought it from the States. And so on....

Fortunately, there were neighbors in the building with whom we could interact in a more pleasant way. On our floor, the *deuxième étage* – the equivalent of the third floor in the U.S.A., with four apartments, there was the flaming redhead Mme Lambert and her family. Mme Lambert ran the tennis club across the street, and was an invaluable source of information and tickets to the Roland Garros French Open tennis tournament each year – one of the four Grand Slam Tennis events around thc world – which I came to value as a marvelous two weeks in late May for sitting in the arenas and watching until sunset the likes of Andre Agassi of Colorado, and Jim Courier, a crowd favorite; Mary Pierce, half American, half French thus a great favorite of the French; and the great Steffi Graf from Germany. Those evenings at Roland Garros were so much more calm and beautiful than the U.S. Open at Forest Hills in Queens. Reminded me of the tranquility, despite the tension, at the U.S. National Doubles Tournament I used to go to as a teenager at the Longwood Cricket Club in Brookline, Massachusetts.

My best friend in the building at 33 was Jacques Chevalier, a former actor who by then was doing voice-overs to earn a living. Jacques opened up his apartment to us whenever we needed a word of advice in French or English, or just a word of welcome. He and his family, consisting of Laurent his wife and Olivia his daughter, would be an important part of our lives for the next eight years, as we took on the bankers, the utilities, and especially the hated *fonctionnaires*, the despised civil servants who ran the country but were untouchable, people with whom we had in any event to deal for visas, cartes d'identité, etc.

Jacques had grown up during World War Two with his actress mother close by his side. He had from early on a mellifluous voice that suited his acting style, and he and I were known as regulars after a while in the neighborhood, especially at the Parks Boulevard Bistrot where we ate a lunch almost weekly together. The Parks Boulevard had excellent home-style cooking, such as coq au vin and boeuf bourguignon, with an excellent selection of wines with which to cleanse the palate, before, during, and after the meal. Jacques helped me develop my taste in French wines and in excellent but moderately priced lunches. He was on a fixed retirement income largely with occasional bumps in monthly income based on royalty payments from earlier films or voice-overs. Sometimes I would buy the meal, sometimes Jacques would when he received payment of a royalty for his voice over work - it seemed to work out as one of us usually had enough money to manage, albeit at times with some effort.

Jacques had a problem with alcohol, he simply drank too much too often. Always wine, sometimes whiskey, and he did indulge in a cognac or two after our lunches. His drinking was a problem for Laurent and Olivia, and I was, as a physician-friend, often called upon late at night to help pour him into bed. They were really warm and welcoming people to me and my wife Deborah and our son Noah. Olivia understandably despised Jacques' drinking and had a hard time accepting her father throughout her adolescence and well beyond, and even to this day. I had trouble with her attitude of intolerance towards him, despite understanding her embarrassment as we strained regularly to get him into bed.

The irony, of course, is that Jacques was a cultured man, with a passion for Debussy, and Berlioz and the *Lieder* of Schumann. He had a love of opera, especially Bizet and French opera; and was a reader of Cartesian philosophy. As an actor, Jacques had a fondness also for American films and American actors, especially Robert Mitchum. During our eight years at 33, Jacques was trying to write a book on the cinema and the great actors and actresses of French and American cinema, many of whom he knew personally. He was, however, unable to publish the book because it had so many pictures which made the cost prohibitive for any publisher.

Last time I saw Jacques was several years ago just before I left Paris. He was by then installed in his own room in a home for retired actors and musicians in Neuilly, a suburb of Paris. When I came up to his room he was listening to Bach – Johan Sebastian, he reminded me – and putting his books into a bookcase provided by the home. Several of those books were books I had written and that made me prideful. We walked about what had been a glorious old estate before becoming a retirement home. Jacques introduced me to certain fellow retirees whom he had met, one or two of whom he even liked. His comment about one resident was striking, more characteristic of his reaction to his cohabitants. "She listens to Sibelius, can you imagine that?"

Meanwhile, Jacques' wife divorced him – for financial reasons, she told him but which I could not believe – while his daughter brought his grandchildren only on special occasions to see him, the legacy, I think, from the misery inflicted on her and her mother by Jacques' frequent drunken episodes.

The one thing I regretted to some extent at 33 was that the life there was decidedly Parisian bourgeois. It was neither highly refined nor particularly bohemian. I suppose I was moving in those years to a life of the literary mind, a life in which writing was beginning to become the priority of my working life. The studies we had had in mind to do with Hôpital Saint Louis as our base were slow to develop because the funding was hard to come by. The governments of the Eastern European countries involved were not interested in having us document the abuses of the health and welfare of their peoples – once these health effects were documented the public pressure would have increased for the governments to provide for better conditions in the mines, to diminish the use of fetal-toxic and carcinogenic pesticides and such on the farms, and to clean up the factories engaged in manufacturing toxic chemicals. And, given the financial constraints these governments had in the days soon after the collapse of the Soviet Union such pressures would be impossible for them to respond to. The entire scientific infrastructure in some of these countries needed to be rebuilt, a generation of new scientists trained, a generation of older scientists retrained. My colleagues and I came to see that we were, in effect, trying to get resources from governments whose resources were so severely limited they had to be used in providing vital public services not in scientific training and research.

Further, living in Paris did something else for me, to me. As it became clear that the work of the Comité International sur L'Environnement et La Santé was ill-starred, the life of the almost -writer began to form itself in my mind, under the influence of a steady barrage of afternoons in the local cafes spent writing at my laptop, and evenings listening to the talk shows involving writers whose names I had come to recognize. With the respect and honors given to artists generally in Paris and to the winners each year of the writing awards, the Prix Goncourt, the Prix Femina, Prix Medicis, etc, I was then in a world in which the creative mind and the written word were valued as nowhere I had ever lived.

I set up a writing table in the dining area of our small apartment at 33, looking out at the courtyard with its single maple tree. In addition to writing in cafes in the neighborhood and elsewhere, I began to sit at the table and write most afternoons. I continued for a while with the work of the Comité but decided finally that it was hopeless, the funds were just not there. AND I really wanted to see if I could write a book, a non-medical, non-scientific book. I wanted to see if I could sit before the so-called "blank" computer page, day after day after day and write. That was not a given. I needed to persuade myself that I had it in me.

Certainly, being an ex-pat in Paris offered up a lot of material, though my whole life was, in fact, available to me for touchstones. I thought that writing an essay-type book about the French gardienne; about the bankers who regularly regulated and watched over the accounts of this American doctor; about my neighbors across the courtyard who played tennis and smoked out their windows; about what it was like for an American working with the *fonctionnaires* attempting to get a long-term Carte de séjour so as to stay legally in France - those sorts of adventures might, if humorously told, in a spirit of affection for La Belle France make for enjoyable reading. These stories led to my first non-medical book, "Tales of an American Émigré in Paris", published by the Editions des Ecrivains in Paris in 2000.

I gave considerable thought to the question of whether to search for a Literary Agent to represent me in submitting this modest debut tome to publishers in the United States and elsewhere. It was a decision I had to make each time I wrote and developed a book. The literary world is replete with tales of writers searching for years for a publisher to market and publish their work. In the year 2000 I had turned 66 and I decided that I did not wish to spend a serious portion of the years ahead of me waiting for acceptances which might or might not come. And so I chose, then and later, as many writers do - and did in past times - to circumvent the process, find a reasonable way to get "Tales" into print and from there into the hands of friends, family and others interested in what I had to say, hoping it would be enjoyed, and letting it go at that. I was not aiming for literary notoriety, or stardom – I had achieved notoriety and stardom as a geneticist and so needed those things not at all. What I hoped was to give a slowly developing cult of readers a pleasant, and/or stimulating few hours of reading enjoyment. For me it was clear that the pleasure of writing the book was the thing that mattered most – and in that "Tales" was a revelation.

Paris did something else for me, for us, something which made me very grateful simply to be there, to stay there and not just pass through while admiring the Tour Eiffel. Paris led to the kind of life which I had but glimpsed briefly earlier in my life - here and there, but mainly in Japan.

In Paris - in the 16th, in St Germain en Laye, and especially later on in the 5[th,] the Quartier Latin - the quality of life became what the quality of life can be. The food, of course, was superb: fresh fruits and vegetables, fresh fowl at the local chicken shop where the poulets, the *dindes* (turkeys), the African-origin *pintade* birds et alia were all fresh and tasteful; ecstacy-inducing cheeses from *fromagiers* whose forebears were at their exact location selling the same cheeses for generations, cheese sellers who knew the difference between a serious brie or fromage bleu and the pasteurized varieties sold en masse in supermarkets. Drink was either a wine of vintage, and a different one for each course, including the sauternes with the foie gras, the Sancerres white or red with the fish and meats, and the cognac at the end of dinner to slake the palette.

For a person with a sweet tooth like mine the presence of chocolatiers in every neighborhood, and of patissiers whose Bûches de Noel would highlight Christmas dinners across the City made Paris radiate a kind of lightness that helped ease whatever pain I might have felt from the often weighty talk with guests at dinners and from the occasional pang at being far from "home" in the U.S.

On Tuesdays and Fridays, the fish monger lady appeared in my neighborhood and I learned a whole new vocabulary, about thick white fishes like *lotte* (monkfish), *bar* or *lieu,* to large species of *maquereau* (mackerel) or *saumon* (salmon), to fresh oysters and snails of all sizes, to eel and sardines which came not in small cans but consisted of two or three finger-lengths of oily dark flesh. Madame educated me to the seasonal variation in the appearance of different fishes, as well as to which fish were to be eaten, by custom, at each holiday time – a rigidity from which one dared not deviate.

But it was not just the food that gave pleasure. The talk at table was expected, with guests but even without invited guests, to be serious and lively. The French enjoy their talking, whether on television, especially later in the evenings when literary talk and political chatter abound; but more importantly in their daily lives, developing such dialogue into an art form. As fast food increasingly thrives among the young, the older generation persists in demanding discourse that can be exhausting for its participants as it was at times for us Americans unaccustomed to it, but the talking is a sine qua non for a successful evening meal at home or in a neighborhood bistro. This emphasis on talking was instrumental in helping my young son become what he would become intellectually. And my wife and I came to love, if not need, those discussions of politics, literature, philosophy.

In contrast, my quiet time came perhaps more naturally and easily. I spent hours each week sitting on "my" bench in the elegant Luxembourg Garden – there are parks and gardens everywhere in France, islands of tranquility in seas of busyness - across from our apartment in the Fifth by the white marble statue of George Sand, to hours spent in the Café Luxembourg nearby sipping espressos, and reading or thinking ad lib but talking only to the waiter to place my order. Similarly, the courtyard at the ancient Hôpital Saint Louis served faculty and myself as a respite from the frenetic world of biomedical research. So the peace that came with daily life in Paris was perfect for an aging ex-scientist - cum writer of fiction. I took inspiration in my writing from the beauty of Paris, of course, but also from the quality of daily life, which gave me pause and comfort as I tried to figure out the next phase of my life. Mainly, though, I enjoyed the moment, just being, as I had done earlier in my life in the Zen gardens of Hiroshima, Nagasaki and Kyoto, especially Kyoto.

Normandy.......To most people in the world, the name "Normandy" connotes the landing sites in France where we Americans and our Allies began, on D-Day, June 6, 1944, the battles to reach Berlin. Images of beach landings and of rows of crosses in military cemeteries are vivid for the "Greatest Generation", as defined by journalist Tom Brokaw. Such images became part of my psyche as well.

But, if you are French, or are living in Paris regardless of your origins, Normandy is a region within a one to two-hour drive from Paris, a region on the English Channel with its cabanas, resort areas, and sandy beaches. We found ourselves in that situation, wanting to know more of France than the Capital, and at the same time wanting to get away on weekends and holidays without committing to a huge travel time.

We began looking and found an ideal town, Bonneville La Louvet, in central Normandy, 30 minutes from Deauville and Trouville, the chi-chi beach resorts of the Greater Paris Region. The *Moulin* – the Mill – was a small house on about two acres of land abutting the Calonne River not far from

Pont L'Evêque. We had stayed one weekend at a charming inn – the *Absinthe* - at the seaside but artsy town of Honfleur on the coast, had met the owner and told her of our interest in finding a rental in this part of Normandy. She (Corinne) in turn knew of a family who owned the small millhouse in Bonneveille La Louvet nearby, and it was available for rent almost immediately. We went to see the little house on the Calonne the very next morning.

From the outset we were amazed at having found this riverside home. A small, somewhat dark three bedroom Normand structure past which the Calonne flowed. The house had been an active mill to which the town *citoy-ens* (citizens) brought their grain to be processed until the 1940's, when the Nazis occupied the town and the house. The Calonne is a tiny rivulet until swollen by rains or flood waters, at which time, as we experienced, it becomes a mighty river. But, I had images of fishing from the riverbank and grilling the fish on the Godin wood-burning stove we would install.

In fact there was no kitchen at all so we had to install one, to make the Moulin habitable. That plus an outside deck above the stream made the Moulin a little piece of paradise, which we faithfully enjoyed on weekends for the next ten years.

Only problem – and it was an issue – was that the humidity engendered by the Calonne led to a highly allergenic state during our weekends. The sneezing would begin with our arrival on Friday evenings and would continue until Sunday afternoons when we would depart. It affected all of us, but especially son Noah. Finally, after those otherwise wonderful years, we scraped some plaster off the walls and voilà! Black mold, thick, ugly and impossible to eliminate. We had tried to buy the Moulin from the (Postel) Family that owned it. We could not reach agreement so we stayed on a while, struggling best we could with nasal discharges and asthma, but we had finally to leave what had become our hideaway. Beautiful in the green summers, rife with the aromas of the apples in the orchard in the fall, while the Calvados was being prepared in nearby Cormeilles. The region was gorgeous with a light white snow in winters - all was good except in spring when the flies and allergies were impossible.

I did do a fair amount of fishing in the river, using all manner of fish as bait; but my family was appalled that I would catch and kill a fish. In the end I had to give up my pastural avocation. Of course I caught mostly eels so not a particularly horrific killing field. And I have to admit that when I grilled the freshly caught eels they were dreadful to the taste: fatty, a bit unctuous, and not much appealing to the palate. It was the fishing itself I loved.

We did, however, enjoy summer outings at Deauville and found the shellfish and other fishes delectable at the Jardin de la Mer in Trouville nearby. I can still taste my favorite plateau de fruits de mer, consisting of shrimp (from small *crevettes* to large succulent *gambas*); gobs of *boulots* (the tiny escargots – wee but delicious); *huitres* (oysters) of many sizes and shapes and origins depending on the time of year); *langoustines* (small lobster-like prawn) and their cousins the *langoustes* that are sweet and succulent and the king of delicacies for the festive seasons and beyond. The plateau for us was accompanied often by a gentle white Sancerre, of proper vintage.

We had these fêtes often in the company of the owners of the Moulin, Marcel and Odile, a warm and friendly couple, native Normands, who lived just outside Honfleur in the family homestead. Marcel was a hard-working gentleman, politically interested and smart beyond his educational background. Odile was a dynamo, always fixing up her houses, yards, and preparing delicious dinners. We would often dine with them at their home or at the Jardin, we were friends. Their only fatal flaw was they loved to come by the Moulin unannounced and spend hours chatting about this or that. Marcel also had stories about the Nazi occupation of Bonneville La Louvet, and he told us of his father's attempts to keep the Nazis off the land, when the Nazis wanted to blow the small bridge which linked the island on which the Moulin sat. It was an adventure, the German Occupation, one they survived but which many obviously did not.

In the end we were so enchanted with our weekend retreat and our friends that we decided to offer to buy the land and the Moulin, so as to have a permanent base in France regardless of where else we might wander. The real estate market was booming at that time in Normandy with hundreds of English coming over each year to buy property. Marcel valued the package at close to 300,000 euros, a figure which we felt was grossly inflated. I offered 200,00 euros, intending to negotiate. Marcel would not, however, reduce his asking price sufficiently to meet us half-way or thereabouts and so the discussions came to naught – except to generate ill will between our families. In the end, as our lease came to its conclusion – it was a classic 3-6-9 French lease, and we had gone the nine years – we decided to stop. We left with some bad feeling on both sides over the failed purchase, and have not remained the longer-term friends we had all anticipated we would. We buried our much-loved bichon Genevieve on the banks of the Calonne where she used to romp freely, among the cows and horses and apple trees. We miss both Genevieve and that marvelous time among the Normands.

In Paris I was finding my way to writing a second book. I had long flirted with the idea of doing a novel, one which would test my creative abilities, unlike the more reportorial book of essays that "Émigré" was. I embarked with trepidation, not knowing if I had it in me to develop characters who would be believable and interesting.

A strange thing happened though en route to writing "Citron's Sonata" (Athena Press, London, 2007).The character of Harry Citron took on a life of his own and I let him do it. Once having defined the limits of his character, I just let him speak and act and it was weirdly satisfying to have created a character who could come up off the page and into the world, my world at least. Not that he was necessarily liked, except by a few, but he was very much alive.

From Chapter One, "…..Over the years Harry often found himself in distant lands, friendless and largely unknown. He was, in fact, content to be in exotic places, places reeking of odors unfamiliar, of faces strange to behold, of names hard to pronounce. He found being in such places, déraciné, much to his liking. He could think his own thoughts more easily, eat whatever new foods appealed to him, go to bed at odd times, and with whomever he pleased, with no need to justify any of it. There was a certain advantage to feeling unencumbered, even if he was not completely so."

Harry's story was complicated because he was a complicated man - but interesting to write and read about. His career, his loves, his wanderings, all very absorbing for me and, I hoped, for those who would read about him.

During that time in Paris I had begun to frequent a small bookshop, The Village Voice, in the Sixth Arrondissement, on a small street, rue Princesse, run by a marvelous and knowledgeable woman named Odile Houlier. Her shop was on two floors - a ground floor and a mezzanine - at 6, rue Princesse, just down from Boulevard Saint Germain. The shop had tables and bookcases laden with new books that reflected Odile's expertise and love for contemporary Anglo-American writing. She founded the bookshop as a bookshop/café in 1981-82, but was overwhelmed by the demands of the food preparation side of the enterprise and gave that up after a couple of miserable years to devote herself to her real love, the books themselves.

Odile told me, one gray Parisian winter afternoon, about her origins. Her parents were French, and her father was an officer in the French Army at the time of the outbreak of WWII. He was arrested and sent to a detention camp from which he escaped, becoming thereafter a member of the French Resistance. Odile's mother went to Drancy on one of the last trains out, and their apartment was taken over by Nazi officers. The Nazis examined her father's books, objected to the Karl Marx writings and to the books by and about the extreme rightist General Lyautey. The Nazis threw all of Houlier's books out onto the street and burned them all.

While Odile had not even been born at that time, she shared her father's outrage at these events, and part of her lifelong love of the written word stemmed, she felt, from what the Nazis had done in their book-burning rage.

I showed Odile my new book, "Citron's Sonata," and she asked to read it right away. A few days later she wondered if I would be willing to do a reading at the Village Voice. I had hoped my Harry would interest her and so I was delighted she thought he (and I) merited the reading.

Readings at the Voice were well attended and very animated. Odile had a following, as did many of the writers who read there. She asked if I would invite members of the Harvard Club of France, a group in which I was active, and I did so, getting an enthusiastic response ahead of the reading from my friends around Paris. I was aware that Odile had been host in her bookshop to some of the best writers of our generation: Raymond Carver, William Gaddis, Richard Ford and Michael Ondaatje had all read from their works upstairs on the mezzanine. Odile had me prepare a flyer she could put up in the window of the Voice, replete with my picture, and a copy of the cover of "Citron's Sonata."

As the mid-February evening of my presentation drew near, I became really anxious. I had had lots of experience at public speaking of course, about genetics and environmental issues, and had been on numerous television shows, including McNeill - Lehrer and many other shows with large audiences. So I was no stranger to "appearing." But this was something very different and I was moderately unhinged. I tried to understand it. I concluded that while genetics and the environment could be spoken about as facts, as hard science even in the presence of disagreement about interpretation of the facts, reading from my own novel was a very different matter. This was my soul on the line – I had exposed some of my innermost thoughts and feelings in the course of writing this book, and at a reading from the book before an audience of literary people I would be laid bare. Further, I would of course be expected to answer questions about the behavior of my characters, their morality, their actions.

With a smattering of Harvard people and friends, like Christopher Larsen, plus the usual Village Voice regulars, the imposing crowd of 60 -70 people crammed onto the upstairs space at 6, rue Princesse at 7 pm on a February night in 2008. I had selected three or four passages to read, and then girded myself to answer questions, led by our host Odile Houlier. It became evident at once that not only had Odile read Harry closely, but most attendees had as well. We discussed Harry's first love Suzanne's stay at the nunnery in Bruges; the infidelity of Anne Marie, Suzanne's daughter and Harry's ultimate lover, who questioned Harry's fathering of Lily; and Harry's reasons for returning to die in a nursing home in Boston. I answered best I could but was delighted that Harry had made such an impression on all these readers. They were really in it with old Harry.

Odile sold a goodly number of copies of "Citron's Sonata", with the store manager, the highly literate Irishman Michael Neal who had filmed the event, on duty at the cash register.

Twelve of us had a dinner after the question and answer period at a local bistrot, *Les Editeurs*, a *café littéraire*, nearby at the Carrefour de L'Odeon in Saint-Germain des Pres. We talked and drank and ate for hours on the leather couches and seats at Les Editeurs. I was delighted both at the interest in Harry and at my own pleasure in the evening's festivities. To have walked and written where Hemingway trod and wrote was, well, one of my life's finer pleasures.

In the months and years that followed Odile faltered : sales began to plummet as e-commerce, i.e. Amazon, took hold. People, even Parisians, ordered their books increasingly from Amazon and, with the appearance of the Kindle, they even began ordering their "books" from cyberspace. Amazon provided books quicker than Odile could deliver them if the book was not already in stock - Amazon books in Europe came very rapidly from the Amazon warehouse in Germany - but at the Village Voice buyers had to pay the VAT, Value Added Tax, which was not required of Amazon buyers. The ultimate blow was delivery of texts directly onto iPad-like devices like Kindle and Nook. To add further to Odile's burdens as a bookseller, she could not by French Law - the so-called *Loi Lang* - reduce prices more than five percent to respond to the invasion of big booksellers who could and did reduce prices significantly especially during seasonal sales.

Additionally, and no small part of Odile's disillusionment after 30 years at rue Princesse, was that serious literature was being rapidly subsumed by the mass-market sensibility, or lack of sensibility, which catered to pure entertainment on a large scale. Odile came to miss the "serious books written from the soul of an author, "as she put it. Literary books were destined for a smaller and smaller portion of the reading public.

Books spoke to Odile Houlier, one of the last great booksellers. And one of the last great readers. She was not a saleswoman, so much as an artist in her own right. The book of a serious author nourished its readers, she felt, and maybe even changed its readers in perceptible ways, freeing their imaginations, allowing the readers to wander beyond their own geographical limits. And beyond their own lives. To Mme Houlier a book was not entertainment – it was a serious, often life-changing experience. Written from the soul of an author for the soul of a reader. A book is not simply a "product" to be mass marketed - at least not for one such as she.

On July 31, 2012, the Village Voice closed its doors, some three years after we left Paris. I mourn its passing still.

The decision to leave Paris and return to the U.S. was much harder for me than the decision to go to Paris had been. It was somehow easier for Deborah. But I sat for many an hour thinking in the Jardin de Luxembourg across from our apartment, communing with the writer George Sand (the white marble statue of her sits opposite the bench I frequented). I did not really want to leave Paris, I adored the life, the daily event was a pleasure. Our apartment on Boulevard Saint Michel in the 5th arrondissement – the *Quartier Latin* - was spacious and centrally located just up the street from the Sorbonne. I was writing productively, had a few friends, and felt physically and mentally well where I was.

But being an ex-pat of long-standing – almost 20 years – had had its implications family-wise. My Mother had died at 93 while I was in Paris, try as I could to be back to Boston often, especially in her final months at the Rehab Center. The Parkinson's had been relentless and she had struggled gamely. She and I knew the end was near. I played a CD she loved of the very beautiful but sad Samuel Barber *Adagio for Strings* at her bedside in her waning days. And she never wavered in trying to ensure that "all the juice was squeezed from the orange" by the time of her death. I was not present at her death; and while I came quickly back from Paris it was not precisely what she had wanted.

My two dear Uncles had passed, one at 92 and one more recently at 88. They had helped to raise me, and were very precious to me; but they had children of their own, my first cousins, and so my sense of guilt at not being there at their endings was a bit muted. I came back from France as soon as I could, helping to bury one but not in time for the other.

The final death of those nearest and dearest was Mother's sister Francis. She had never had children, though married many years. I was very close to her, almost but not quite her surrogate child. When I decided to move to France, she and her husband had removed me from my position as Executor of their considerable estate in a move that was punitive as much as it was practical. Once her husband passed my wife and I looked after Francis best we could from afar, had her to our Normandy moulin, which she loved, though physically hard for her to manage given her visual difficulties – macular degeneration et alia – and her heart disease. We spent holidays with her in Boston, returning often to help oversee her affairs. At her last Thanksgiving, I cooked a turkey in her apartment on Beacon Street for our small family and, while she enjoyed it, and managed to come to the table, her words on biting into the bird were memorable: "I like my turkey hot, Dear. Please remember for next year." She died shortly thereafter, an inspiration to us all, full of the life force until the very end of her 96 years.

It was not only death that worked its will on us: my seven cousins and I grew apart. They had their own spouses, careers, and children and while I saw them all from time to time during my twenty years away - one cousin and his family even visited briefly in Paris and we had a lunch on the Champs Elysees - there was an inevitable gap which no amount of emailing could bridge.

The effect of this distancing on my own older three children was unspoken but the absent father was now truly absent - in constant contact, but they were in their twenties and thirties by that time and living what I felt were pretty much independent lives. They each came to Paris from time to time and I saw them, of course, when I returned to the States several times a year; but the price they paid, even as adults, for my being an ex-pat is hard to assess. We are together often now that I am back to stay, and we are very close, but those years were costly.

Perhaps my greatest concern about returning to the States was that a return might endanger my writing. I felt that in the United States I was a physician, a scientist, and my serious writing was done in Paris. My identity as a physician, albeit a genetical physician, an academic physician, was firmly ensconced in the psyches of family, friends, and most of all in my own mind. For that reason I felt shaky in returning - not just because I was so content in France with our way of life, but because the reality was two books written and published (*"Essays of an American Émigré.."* and *"Citron's Sonata")*, but a third was on its way - a collaborative effort with dear friends from Haym Salomon AZA, "From Neighborhood to Manhood: The Boys of Blue Hill Avenue" (Small Batch Books, Amherst, 2011).

"Neighborhood" was one result of a wondrously warm and loving week seven of my AZA friends and their wives spent with us in a combined Paris-Normandy visit. We oriented the trip for them to our apartment in Saint Germain en Laye, where we lived while Noah attended the Lycee International, and to the Moulin in Normandy - a visit highlighted by our walking through the cemetery at Colleville sur Mer overlooking Omaha Beach and the Channel, where the 10,000 Yanks killed on or about D-Day were buried. Row on row of crosses with an occasional Star of David breaking the pattern is something we and they will never forget.

The idea for our tight-knit group to write a series of autobiographies came to us then, putting down on paper some of what we meant to one another. It was not easy for the Alephs to write about their lives since Dorchester and Roxbury, but with encouragement some of them persisted. The result was "From Neighborhood to Manhood".

As I as Editor wrote in my Introduction to "Neighborhood", "The writers of the autobiographical essays that here follow grew up in the Boston neighborhoods of Dorchester and Roxbury, which ranged from Blue Hill Avenue in Mattapan on one end to Grove Hall and Franklin Park on the other, with the clear center of existence between Morton Street, at Cutler's Pool Hall, and the G and G Delicatessen, several blocks away. We went to the Hebrew Schools in the area; were Bar Mitzvahed in its synagogues; ate our first corned beef sandwiches and half-sour pickles at the G and G, where we would sit for hours whiling away the breaks in our education; hung out in our best suits at "The Wall" of Franklin Field during the High Holy Days, looking for our female counterparts; and later moved our activities over to the nearby Hecht House, as we progressed through high school and approached college.

"All this while our fathers worked to make a living, sometimes but rarely with financial help from our mothers, whose role it was in life more commonly to keep the kosher household and prepare for Shabbat and the High Holidays, while raising us as proper Jewish children. Life in that Dorchester and Roxbury was not easy, but it had the inestimable virtue of bringing us close together in our families – though not always – and to our friends outside the family. The struggle just to get by financially, emotionally, was difficult for many of us and especially for our parents, but out of that struggle came a set of values that honed our survival skills and made us strong for our lives to come."

During the visit of my friends with us in Paris and Normandy, and in the subsequent putting together of the series of autobiographical essays for "Neighborhood," I came to understand that the values learned in Dorchester and Roxbury were still very much a part of me. The closeness of family and friends as I grew up remained very important to me. I had wandered for a lifetime, far and wide to be sure; but this re-awakening of feelings acquired in earlier days could not be ignored. As I sat at my writing desk in Paris and in the neighborhood cafes I frequented, I came to feel a deep-seated ache. I was forced to acknowledge to myself the need to return to family, friends, and country.

My main concern about returning was what the impact of the return would be on my writing.

In the States I was and felt very much a physician, and others saw me that way. Here in Paris I was no longer a physician, had given up that part of my life. I was now simply a writer of books - three down and a fourth on the way - and I felt good, as they say, in my new skin. The books might have been good or bad, read by modest-sized audiences, and I may have published them at my own expense. But, truth was, none of that mattered: I had written them and that was, for me, the miracle of Paris.

However much my anxiety level rose about my ability to continue doing in the U.S. what I was doing in Paris with the writing, there developed a certain inevitability to our departure. Further, and importantly, my wife did not want to die and be buried in a foreign country, a point of view vastly premature given the difference in our ages. She felt strongly that it was time to go back "home". And, with our son Noah no longer in France, the argument was a hard one for me to win, even though I welcomed the idea of being buried in Père La Chaise or, better, at Montparnasse, with its bevy of distinguished writers and other artists. Up the street from where we lived in the Quartier Latin, the cemetery at Montparnasse houses the remains of Dreyfus, Baudelaire, de Maupassant, Sartre and de Beauvoir, not to mention Piaf and Chopin and even the American Jim Morrison.

But, such was not to be. I concluded when all was said and done that I was now strong enough to go on writing anywhere: It was my commitment to myself - I was no longer a conflicted Harvard undergraduate.

13

On Being a Writer

I returned with trepidation, I admit, to America. Trepidation about whether I could continue to write freely, of course, but what I feared more was the materialism of America. In France, while there was a certain amount of emphasis on wordly goods, on the acquisition of things, it was nothing compared with that of my native land, as I remembered it. To much of the world, including my countrymen, France has always been wine from Bordeaux and haute cuisine second to none. But Gordon Gekko's "Greed is good" was not something the French nor I could accept – ever. Further, we were in France when W Bush became President, and that was, well, awkward; it was really an embarrassing time to be an American abroad. Trump, of course, is still worse.

The contemporary heroes of France were and are not entrepreneurs but writers and intellectuals, on the one hand, like Jean d'Ormesson of the Academie francaise, and rugged individualists like Johnny Hallyday the Rocker, on the other. They had become my heroes, too.

And so, while I was excited to come home to the land of my birth, my family, land of my childhood, my education and my successes, I was fearful, too, and not just about the writing. I had changed, grown closer to my more basic instincts.

First stop back: Vermont. My wife began a company in Vermont devoted to English-language education. She had been actively involved in language education while in France, and, upon our return, she based her company in Vermont where we had enjoyed many a vacation while coming from abroad. Middlebury in particular was appealing because of the University there and the nearby rivers, streams and mountains. I also discovered a coffee shop where I could happily go each afternoon and write, along with others, sometimes to chat, while sipping decent espressos.

The owner turned out to be a gentleman from Central Massachusetts, and John hosted readings with the local *New England Review*, a Middlebury College-based writers' journal that held regular readings at his coffee shop every other month. John himself did not write, but he had wandered to Vermont and established the coffee shop, Carol's Hungry Mind, as part of his life, not just to earn a livelihood but to live out his dream of how life should be lived, in the country, the educated country, the unpretentious country.

At first the marvels of Vermont living were very appealing. The summers were warm and the wildlife plentiful – including the bears who frequented our otherwise isolated grounds. The fall, of course, was beauteous with the foliage of the sugar maples being unparalleled in reds and yellows and all manner of colors in between. The winter was a different matter, beautiful but rugged and hard to manage.

As the seasons passed I found myself onto a different

kind of writing: I was now doing short stories and that felt really comfortable. The plots of my stories were relatively simple, the characters interesting in their activities, and I could mold the stories to whatever length I wished. I did a novella or two, but mostly kept the stories to five to fifteen pages of text. The stories reflected my time in France but more often I found they were based on earlier periods in my life in Boston, among family and friends.

The Editor of the *New England Review* was a patron of Carol's Hungry Mind and he and I talked of my writings and, after he had read a story or two of mine, he invited me to do a reading at its writers' series at Carol's that May. I selected a short story about an elderly woman in a nursing home whose resident boyfriend was affectionate beyond the low tolerance of the nursing staff for such manifestations of affection among its patients. There were gasps of recognition in the audience as I spun this story

The second tale was a piece yet more fully out of my imagination, about a lonely man named Freddie who was a backgammon player in the City. Freddie met online a woman named Josephine, with whom he fell further in love when he met her in person. The story tells of their life together. Then, Freddie had a dream one night. Freddie "... decided to become a frog, to sit in the sun by day, to copulate by night. Being a frog in the city was impossible, and so Freddie decided to go to the country to find a pond. There Freddie discovered a lady frog and they had lots of tadpoles and Freddie was happy. After a few years of it, though, Freddie decided to leave the pond - he was bored. But he could not just leave; he had all these tadpoles to look after.

And so he decided to be a frog at night, and something else, not sure what, he would find something satisfactory - during the day. And then Freddie woke up."

The stories were well received in the coffee shop that warm May evening by the Middlebury Common, and the audience wanted more of this material, which encouraged me greatly.

One afternoon that summer I asked John how his shop had gotten its name. He told me the sad tale: how he and his wife Carol were preparing the shop for its opening, doing the last-minute cleaning up and the painting of the walls, when Carol complained of severe fatigue. She went to a local physician who could not find much of anything, and asked her to return if symptoms persisted. A week later Carol collapsed and died, at age 48. Cancer of the pancreas was found at autopsy.

John mourned for many months but finally opened the coffee shop as he felt Carol would have wanted.

After a year or two, John hooked up with another woman, a local, named Irene, also about 50 and he was en route to a recovery from his wife's death. John and Irene loved to ski, and they went up to Killington the next winter. Irene bent over to tie her ski boots on and she keeled over, dead.

By the time John and I met some three or four years after these events he had recovered enough to be reasonably content. The coffee shop had become a success, mostly because he was outgoing and personable despite all. He met and lived with another woman, skied and hiked in Vermont as prescribed for his mental and physical health, and enjoyed the largely literate clients who frequented his shop.

I continued writing in Vermont and was relieved that writing now seemed a part of me wherever I was, I need not worry. But Vermont was perhaps too radically different from Paris to allow me to be comfortable. One story I wrote in those years, "Vermont Girl," catches the spirit of the place as I felt it.

"Elsa was born in Bellingham, a town of 2,330 souls, almost but not quite all farmers. The town was situated in the Green Mountains, just west of where Robert Frost used to hang out.......Some of the children from these farm homes in Vermont had gone to college and moved on to the bigger cities of Burlington, Rutland, and even out of State, working in Information Technology. But not Elsa. She was a farm girl through and through, loved raising sheep, baking breads, and selling fresh eggs from her chickens at the Saturday morning Farmers' Market in the center of Bellingham, a Market known for its excellent fresh produce and its sometimes brilliant crafts - the rug hookers and quilters were artisans apart from the purveyors of fresh pork and fruit pies."

I had thought that Carol's might save me, but it closed at five - people retreated in winter especially but all year in actuality. Vermonters generally went home for a six o'clock or earlier dinner while the Middlebury students were ordered by the Dean to stay on Campus for safety reasons, and not go downtown to Carol's or to the movie theater or anywhere else. Thus all shops in Middlebury closed around five o'clock to reflect the ways of the students and of the early-to-bed farmers. Many an evening we caught a seven o'clock show at the cinema, and there were perhaps five or six others in the whole theater, and that was a crowd!

So, what I at first found charming in its silences and peacefulness became, as time went on, painful isolation. While we had returned from Paris to a naturally beautiful place, Middlebury, Vermont, was not the kind of civilization I/we required. I continued with my writing, true, and that was a great comfort to be sure; but there was a singular lack of amenities that a city, even a somewhat larger city, would offer. Plus the winters were utterly brutal. I did not expect Paris in the Green Mountains but I also did not wish to feel prematurely buried.

One very cold, snowy evening in Ripton, where we lived just outside of Middlebury, we decided to head south, to visit our son and a few friends who wisely spend winters in warmer climes. I found online a "winter rental" at an idyllic-sounding place called Ibis Isle, part of the Palm Beach area on Florida's southeast coast.

I have never been attracted to Florida, but in the January winter of the Northern New England which was Vermont, South Florida seemed very appealing, indeed. Upon arrival, as described in my story entitled "Ibis Isle" there were, "… herons, pelicans, flamingoes and assorted other birds along with the ibises, which take advantage of the grove trees and the tides of the intracoastal waters to eat and to breed – above all to breed. As you drive over the bridge that joins the island to the mainland, there are fishermen with lines in the waters below, catching an occasional snapper or grouper. Some of these fishermen are wizened old men with corn cob pipes extruding from the corners of their mouths. Others are much younger, lads who have inherited from their grandfathers the gene for a leisurely day's fishing off the bridge. For some, I suppose, what they catch – the Catch of the Day – is dinner."

And, "I wandered around this gorgeous island in the intracoastal, from my building marked 'Chateau Chantilly,' to the 'Chateau Versailles,' next door, to the 'Chambour' beyond, all the while walking my dog morning, noon and night."

I go on here in the tale to describe why Joel, my main character, was there on Ibis Isle. I shared with Joel his feeling about being there, when he says ".. the casting of the line into the waters below is appealing.....(but truth is) my bones are weary and need resurrection via the warmth of the sun. While life has been kind to me in many ways, I am worn out, no other way to put it. I have lurched from professional gig to professional gig, making a buck....... then chucking it and working ..... in various parts of the world. Now I wanna just breathe easy, sip easy, inhale or not as I please......Further, I have lot of reading I want to do in the peace and silence of the days and nights yet to come. I like the Great Books but even more the fiction of my time. Having done the Hemingway stuff and the Fitzgerald stuff, I am anxious to see how more recent writers see the world - writers like Carver, now passed; Toibin, in full force over in Brooklyn; Eggers, nouveau arrivé in New York; and best of all, Cormack McCarthy of Southwest fame".

So while I was escaping the Vermont winter, I did have another agenda in mind. I had a son Robert with whom to spend time, friends to catch up with there, and, like Joel, my own soul to warm in the Florida sun, while writing more stories like the ones I had read at Carol's Hungry Mind. Also, I could live a more physically and mentally active life than in the bitter cold and deep snow of Middlebury. In fact, I began on Ibis Isle to put together my first collection of stories.

Eventually, I selected 15 tales I felt were of reasonable quality and tried to put them together for another book. Were these stories in any way linked, one to the other? I searched retrospectively for a link but came to feel that any attempt to claim that a tie-in existed would have been artificial and so I concluded that the book was simply a series of independent tales. Written in Paris, Middlebury, Florida and Boston, the stories were assembled in a more or less random fashion and I published them, with the Harvard Book Store in Cambridge and with Amazon as "Last Man Standing: Stories" (2014).

They sold reasonably well and were very favorably reviewed by colleagues and friends, which pleased me greatly inasmuch as I felt people were genuinely enjoying them. I did another reading in Florida at the home of a friend, where a journalist – Ron Wiggins - from the Palm Beach Post compared the stories favorably to the work of William Saroyan, enthusiastically asking for more.

After the cold weather had passed up north; after we had tolerated the humidity of the Florida summer poorly; and after my time with my older son and friends felt "up" for the time being, September came neigh and we prepared to head north to Boston. Florida was, in the end, a refreshing hiatus but not an end point for us though we considered it: despite the beauty of the ocean, the somewhat gentler pace of life and the warmth of friends and family it did not feel like home and I suppose that is an intangible that must be dealt with in the making of such decisions as to where to live. The idea of Boston, finally, where life for me at least had begun seemed very appealing.

We did not do it especially well, however. We took an apartment in the much-changed South End - much-changed for the better from what the South End was like when I was growing up in Boston - and drove north to a place we took sight unseen, on old Saint Botolph Street.

The advantages of the location were considerable: near two of my foremost Boston loves, the Boston Public Garden - where as a younger man I used to ice skate in winter, ride the swan boats in summer, and stroll while appreciating the flowers the rest of the year - and the Boston Public Library, a wonderful hallowed old structure in Copley Square, where I often studied and wrote an occasionl research paper while at the Latin School. Of course, the Library has been updated, modernized, and now has all manner of computers, CD's, records, digitized films, etc, and a fancy coffee shop, but it also has preserved its former ambiance for the likes of me. Also, the Boston Arena was farther up St. Botolph Street, where the Bruins played many a hockey game and open skating was plentiful on weekends for the rest of us.

Nowadays, I knew, the Square has become home to numerous fancy hotels, like the Westin, the Marriott. Even the Copley Plaza is no longer the Copley Plaza but is now the Fairmont Copley Plaza with, sadly, no afternoon tea in the lobby as in olden times. The many restaurants in the neighborhood serve all manner of lobsters, steaks, et al, and one will never want for a coffee given all the Starbucks shops and other coffee shops in the 'hood. A big Barnes and Noble – with coffee shop of course – is the centerpiece of the Prudential Mall so books too, a staple of the neighborhood for centuries, continue to be available for purchase but in a different guise.

For me there was yet another dimension: the spirits of my deceased relatives poked their heads around almost every corner of the South End, since it was an area I frequented with one or another of them at one time or another: the iced-over pond in the Boston Gardens where Uncle Sam and I would go on a winter's day; Jordan Hall where Aunt Francis took me to Pinocchio and to Sleeping Beauty; the Symphony Hall where Uncle Edward bought me my first subscription to the Thursday after-school children's concerts, where I first listened to Ravel's Bolero and Schubert's Unfinished Symphony; and the Zionist House on lower Commonwealth Avenue where Mother worked and where she and I would share a sandwich now and again while sitting on a bench on her lunch hour.

So returning to Boston was a pleasure of multiple dimensions to this ex-Latin School boy.

But the apartment we took sight unseen before driving up to Boston from Ibis Isle proved to be an expensive disaster. It was small to a fault, the Vermont furniture would not fit, and the price per square foot was exorbitant. I did manage to write a few stories but the scene was unpleasant, compounded by our by then two dogs – one was the minipoodle Rico who was sweet but yappy and nervois; the other was Noah's Olde English Bulldog Jacques who was a puppy but growing daily, laid in our lap unexpectedly because Noah was off and away to Southeast Asia for a long, slow journey.

Our neighbors in Boston lived very closely next to us, on all sides, and the dogs were, well, not quiet especially when we went out and left them for a few hours. After almost a year, as our lease was about to expire, and with another Boston winter coming, wisdom dictated a retreat southward to warmer climes with more space. And so it was to a cabin in the Great Smokey Mountains of Tennessee that we emigrated, a cabin which the wife had fixed up and planned to sell.

After a three-day drive southward from Boston, through some of this country's most beautiful land - the Blue Ridge Mountains of Virginia, and the foothills of the Great Smokies - we arrived in a world I had only read about. The central and southeastern portion of the Appalachian Mountains is home to about 25 million people, and includes in purest form the northern part of Eastern Tennessee, the northwestern part of North Carolina, plus central Kentucky. These are "moonshine" states with a history of feuding clans and lots of poverty. Appalachia as a distinctive cultural region involves some 13 states but the Eastern Tennessee area is perhaps the prototype.

I would read a lot during our stay there about the Cherokees, especially about Sequoyah otherwise known as George Gist, a self-educated and literate Cherokee whose statue adorns the dome of our Congress in Washington, D.C mainly for his contributions to Cherokee Nation. The Cherokee were forceably moved by Andrew Jackson and colleagues from Tennessee who coveted the Indian lands for its timber and coal. The Tennessee Valley Authority in the worst of 20th century times had built the dams which now dot the landscape and make a mess of it.

While there I learned a lot about the history and peoples of Eastern Tennessee, and I did love the Smokies themselves. We drove up to Cades Cove from time to time to see the elk and the bison, and other species that tended to remain at higher elevations. Our cabin was half way up on a mountain road, the only road down or up the mountain where we lived. We would sit out on the deck and feast our eyes on the lush green of the decidual forest which surrounded us, fully leafed in during springtime and summer, with glorious multi-colored trees in the fall. And, in winter we could see the clouds of moisture ringing the peaks and valleys of the Mountains, thus the name Smokies.

I had never before witnessed the phenomenon of these blue-tinted clouds of vapor that just hung in the air all around the Mountains. The mist is said to be caused by vapors arising from the vegetation and humidity of the Mountains, a phenomenon the Cherokees called "shaconage', or place of the blue smoke. It is a complex phenomenon but beautiful for the beholder.

For me the time from arrival in Tennessee - spring 2015 - until the fire that evicted us on November 28, 2016, was a marvelously quiet and creative time. I knew no one in Gatlinburg and did not wish to meet people. The isolation of that time suited me. While my wife and son would be off to work, I was the beneficiary of a peaceful day, my only obligation for long stretches of time being to walk the dogs once in a while but mainly to write, or think about writing.

To be sure, I was enchanted by the natural life around the cabin. As I sat in my study at the far end of the cabin, the occasional family of bears would stroll by just beyond my window. Usually a mother bear and a cub or two or three, heading across our land en route to the deeper forest just beyond. Or, impressively, and much more frightening was the presence of a big black bear, the presumed papa, whose size dwarfed that of the momma and cubs combined! I messed with none of them, simply observed their almost leisurely stroll into the bush, or even sometimes via the paved road down the mountain. They never rushed, they never panicked – something I admire still unto this day.

The squirrels of the Great Smokies were, in contrast, in constant motion: they would race up and down the trees and along the tops of our fences, with acorns in the fall, dashing to their storage bins in trees deeper in the forest.

We had a small stream of water erupting from the midsection of our driveway out front and that rivulet attracted thirsty wild turkeys almost daily. We were on some sort of route for they appeared in considerable numbers at times – it was not unusual for ten or fifteen big turkeys to stroll onto the driveway, peck away at the water, and then gather their smaller ones together and head farther up the hill, silent as the night, en route to God only knows where.

As a youngster growing up in Dorchester I recall no such wildlife, neither in New York nor Paris, and so this was all a considerable treat. I knew about mice, about cockroaches and even deer from Austerlitz, but big black bears? Wild turkeys? All very comforting. I recognize that my responses to animals over the years has evolved. While growing up, I had two failed experiences with dogs – always the allergies I was told, but really, Mother simply did not wish to bother with them, I believe, and understandably so, as she was busy working and was impatient with nonhuman species. We had a marvelous singing canary named Pete when I was young but Pete's time on earth and his place were very circumscribed. The bright yellow canary was the sum of it.

On the other hand, once free of the concern about the likelihood of my going into anaphylaxis upon exposure to dog dander, I became enamored of our bichon frise Genevieve, for whom I was literally prepared to risk my life as she faced probable drowning out at the Moulin in Normandie. I watched as Gen grew old and feeble and finally caved in after 18 totally loving years. Then, after some eight years of mourning, of seriously missing her, we got a minipoodle when in Vermont. He was/is apricot-colored and so in deference to his "aprico"-color in French, we called him Rico. He is the older of the two pet loves of my life. He was with us in Vermont and has been ever since.

In addition, our son bought an Olde English Bulldog puppy while working in California. As mentioned above, when he gave up that financial stuff and set off for Asia, he deposited young Jacques with the 'rents and we have raised him to this day. His personality is like Ferdinand the Bull of my youth: He only wants to stroll among the flowers, sniffing their aromas as he goes. Or he sits on his haunches awaiting the urge to move, which cannot be "encouraged" by the likes of those who care for him. Sometimes I sit and watch Jacques, as he just sits like a Buddha and thinks - he does think, I can tell - and I wonder what is on his mind. But, maybe I am wrong, and there is nil on his mind as the Buddha might have it. Jacques is the enigma, always good to have a being around who makes one stop and ask.

This book began to take shape soon after our arrival in Tennessee. I am not sure why but the undisturbed way of life for me was the key, I think. I had long thought about writing a version of my life story as, first, a medical scientist, and then the story of how I evolved over the years into someone who would write non-science. Part of this tale had to do with where we have wandered all these years, because I do think place and environment have had a serious role in whatever creativity I have expressed. Maybe not *the* key factors but of major importance. The issue is not, was not for me, a room of my own, but rather a life of my own. In Tennessee, maybe as nowhere else thus far I was a lone soul, able to exercise complete self-expression. No one to impress, those to whom I felt answerable were long dead and so I had no one to answer to except myself.

This absence of almost anything recognizable allowed me, forced me, to face myself. The spirits of those who came before fell away and allowed me to look in the mirror in a new way, a better way, a freer way than heretofore. Paris had been life-affirming; Tennessee was for me a void to be filled, by love of the mountains and the animals and the mists. Above all, I filled it with words.

I am grateful that as we moved on after the fire the momentum to write has continued and I have at last become closer to what I have always wanted to be, whether I knew it or not. Suddenly, isolated in Tennessee, the days of work at my desk with an occasional bear passing by and with turkeys in my driveway, along with the blue mist of the Smokies themselves, freed me. And that momentum has continued on to Gloucester much to my relief.

14

Pensées: Home, by the Sea in Massachusetts

Pensées I. Finding Gloucester

They call the High School teams of Gloucester "The Fishermen" and the players proudly wear the colors crimson and white. There is a certain swagger to being a Fisherman, a pride of place, of origin, and I have come to share that pride in recent years. Not because I have been here very long, and not because my roots are here. What it is is that I have cast my lot with the town, feel loyal to it - in just a year or two - and feel at home here in the fishing village on the North Shore of Boston.

I do not totally understand how this came about, this sense of belonging; but I have embraced the feeling and the town. Not that I am much of a fisherman, though I enjoy casting my line in from the shore. Used to do it often growing up in Boston during summer vacations at the beaches to the north and south, especially south, of Boston in Nantasket,

Scituate, and Cohasset. Just as I fished on the banks of the Calonne by the Moulin in Normandy.

But here in Gloucester fishing is a serious business. Downtown by the Harbor Walk there are a series of bronze Memorial plaques with the 5,368 names, dating back to the 1600's, of those who have "gone down to the sea in ships" and not returned. In that time, over 1000 boats have been lost, 265 with all hands. The plaques remind me of the Vietnam War Memorial in Washington, the names go on and on and on. The fishermen were, still are, like the town itself, of Irish, Italian, Portuguese, and Scandinavian origin. One cannot help but feel moved by their spirits as one stands overlooking the harbor, these brave souls who ventured forth out to Georges Bank and beyond to earn a hard-fought living on the ocean. This diversity - not total diversity as there are probably few blacks in their number - is what has given birth to a multicultural, working class town of welcoming, generally tolerant people.

In my teen-age years I would come sometimes from Boston with Mother up to Rockport, just beyond Gloucester, for a few weeks of sunning on a modest beach in the middle of that town, and of strolling by the art galleries that have become in recent years a serious art colony. But Rockport is now for the affluent; Gloucester is still for the fishermen and their families, for the descendants of quarry workers and their families from Finland and Sweden; for the Sicilian - especially the Sicilian - fishermen who also are the creators of coffee shops, restaurants, and bakeries, places one can hear non-stop Italian spoken by construction workers, recent immigrants – still - from Trapani in Eastern Sicily and Taormina and Catania in Western Sicily. On some boats only Italian is spoken. As recently as 1994 to 2001, the Gloucester fishing fleet numbered 1000 vessels; by 2012, that number fell to under 400, the result, most claim, of imposed Federal limits on the number and especially the weight of the NOAA allowable daily catch.

I go to one Café in particular the Café Sicilia, for an afternoon espresso, but I go to the Lone Gull or the Pleasant Street Tea and Coffee House if I want to sit and write for hours as I used to do in Paris.

We live, Deborah and I and our two dogs, at the edge of the Rocky Neck Art Colony where for centuries artists originally from New York and Boston have come to paint, to catch the incredibly brilliant colors off the sea all day and the sky at sunset. Van Gogh would feel at home here.

As for me I feel I can create here, write what is in me, whatever that may be. Here an artist of whatever stripe is valued. We are beyond the bedroom communities of Marblehead and Swampscott, here in Gloucester we are all Fishermen.

I have passed through a life-long period that is made up, as Harry Citron described in Chapter One of "Citron's Sonata", of love for "exotic places, places reeking of odors unfamiliar, of faces strange to behold, of names hard to pronounce." Harry liked being déraciné, as I have until now.

When we returned to the U.S., after almost 20 years where I was déraciné in an alien land, albeit one I loved and love still, we began a different kind of search, not for the exoticism of earlier days – as Harry Citron described it while writing his "sonata" - but a search for a rooting. We wandered, my wife and I, looking for a more or less permanent place. But though we were in our own country, we wandered, wandered even in our own country.

Gertrude Stein stated this dilemma well. She said, "America is my country and Paris is my home town...And so I am an American and I have lived half my life in Paris, not the half that made me but the half in which I made what I made."

I came to understand the issue still more when reading "The Jolly Corner" of Henry James. He wrote about one Spencer Brydon, a fictional 19th century American of means who had lived in Europe for thirty years, and returned full of uncertainty about his native land and what had become of it. I had, as Spencer had, to undergo what James referred to as "repatriation." I took that to mean that return from Europe would be, for me as it was for Spencer Brydon, a process and not a moment in time.

Neither Vermont, nor Florida, nor Tennessee, nor even parts of my own Massachusetts were suitable. I came to feel that one recognizes home only when one finds it - that is, there is no way one can pre-determine where within our Big Country, or in the world, home will be.

Spencer tries in the story to explain these matters to his friend Alice Staverton. But Alice has lived all her life in a house of charm on Irving Place in New York, a few blocks from Spencer's home of origin. She cannot really understand why Spencer did not spend his life in New York as a real estate developer making gobs of money, given the extent of his holdings. But that was not what Spencer (or I) had in mind to do with our lives and so neither of us did that. It was a choice to wander, to discover what and where I wanted to be.

Pensées II. On Friends

After the Gatlinburg Fire of November 2016, I began a period of reflection about friends retained and lost over the years.

Jerry is a guy from Brooklyn who has remained a true pal over the past 30 years. He is a City College guy, a lawyer who practiced in the Bronx. His roots, I should note, are decidedly Orthodox Jewish but in practice he is what we call "Reformed", though I am much more liberal in my religiosity than he. With him any mention of an anti-Israel position on settlements, or on mistreatment of Arab Israelis, and he gets upset with me. He responds with, "Why are you attacking my Grandfathers?" He and his wife Vivienne, a distinguished psychotherapist in Manhattan, had a house not far from ours in the country in Upstate New York, a house she set up very comfortably; but the house was isolated on several acres in the woods and that isolation she did not much like. Jerry, however, dearly loved that house, and just being up there in the Berkshires.

We began to go out all together in the Berkshires for dinners, movies and concerts, which was a joy; and our friendship both as a couple and individually grew during those years. Jerry practiced in the Bronx and we talked a lot about his clients and my patients, without names or identifying remarks. One cold, dark, wintry, Berkshire night Jerry had a serious cardiac episode which he survived but that understandably increased radically his wife's sense of isolation. In the end, Jerry and Vivienne had to sell that house in the woods, much to Jerry's dismay, he loved it so.

Jerry and I can talk, I mean communicate without many reservations, and how often does one have a friend like that? We can bellyache about Cashman and the Yankees – Jerry is really more a Mets fan, he has admitted. AND sin of sins, a Jets fan, while my loyalties are 100 percent Yankees and football Giants. These loyalties, I recognize, are unusual for a Boston Boy.

Okay, the Red Sox of Boston were great when the guys like Ted Williams, Bobby Doerr and Johnny Pesky returned from the War. But, still, a Braves fan like me, even a jilted Braves fan, could not simply shift allegiance to either the Red Sox or, God forbid, to another National League team, could not be done. And so I was a vulnerable teenager, whose baseball idols were Joe Dimaggio, Charlie Keller, and Tommy Heinrich, and Allie Reynolds, there was nothing I could do about that. But that was okay in Jerry's world, a Yankee fan was always welcome.

Now, the Giants of New York were a different story. We had not much of a professional football team in Boston during my pre-Patriot early years, and by the time I got to New York and NYU Medical School, Y.A. Tittle and Frank Gifford were doing heroic things in the Bronx – also in the Bronx – and so that was a relatively easy one, simply filling the void. The clincher came years later when Al Schwarz my father-in-law to be, an avid Giants fan despite his Jersey roots, came back from his days as a Marine in Korea, and was offered, as a returning Vet, season tickets to the Giants; he bought them and they have been a major part of our family's inheritance ever since.

So, a doctor from Dorchester and a lawyer from Brooklyn can become simpatico friends, sharing sports, Tanglewood and the arts, which we have done ever since. But we are simpatico in many ways, mostly in our sensibilities. We read and discuss what we read; we are Democrats to our cores; and we love life, enjoy it in a full-throated way. That love of life is for me a sine qua non of my kind of friendship.

JP has been a friend since our first days at medical school. He was a Midwesterner - Wisconsin – by origin, with an undergraduate degree from Johns Hopkins. JP's father was a well-known pathologist, so JP was savvy medically. On arrival in New York and Medical School he was able to get a studio on the Upper East Side while I was poking around looking for a furnished room. JP took a studio apartment on East 60th Street just off Third Avenue while I "settled" - after a brief stint with Mrs Gratton at Stuyvesant Town - on East 64th Street at Park, for $5 a week, complements of Ben and Cheri. The doctor couple simply wanted someone in their brownstone much of the time with their kids both away at college. So, Jimmy and I were Upper East Side residents, who commuted down to Bellevue each day for classes, labs, etc.

We shared one other trait those first and second years at Medical School: We both found the courses tough and, initially anyway, did not do well. We, as numerous others, made up the core of the anti-Dean's list. I was simply a scientific ignoramus in those days - and as the Dean of Students, William Hubbard, informed me, they took a chance on me because I had "done so well at Harvard" in my major and figured I would catch up scientifically, which I did but was slow to do. Jim came into his own during our clinical years as I did. Thus he and I became close friends, not just in adversity. We also shared a liking for pediatrics, both the pediatric service at Bellevue and the field of pediatrics more broadly. Jim went on to spend his career in the practice of pediatric psychiatry in New York, much loved by patients and their families..

Over the years, after we interned together in pediatrics at Bellevue, roomed together at Bellevue when on call, and we kept in touch as our affection for one another, and our own families, remained strong.

That was not always the case with "friends." I "lost" two pals as life went on: One was a dear friend initially from Hollis Hall our freshman year at Harvard, and later best man at my first wedding. The other was a friend from Johns Hopkins, acquired really during my years in Hiroshima. But the mechanisms for their separation from my sphere of living were different.

At College, Jack and I hung out together, spent hours at the Hayes Bickford Cafeteria then across from Widener Library talking about neutrinos and the rotations of the sun and earth - we were both in a Natural Science requirement-type course. But the main unifying force was "Good and Evil in Western Literature, a course which gave full expression to our philosophical dilemmas of that time. I was pre-occupied with thoughts of suicide in those days, and Jack, while less so as I recall, was munching on Kant and Hegel. We were a sorry lot, two working-class origin young men, he from Akron, I from Dorchester, both very much taken with philosophical issues and our own uncertain futures. Jack ended up at Yale Law School, and went on to be an academic lawyer, with numerous Fulbrights to his name. We drifted apart over the years despite good intentions on both sides, but we have partially reconciled in recent years.

Phil and I first met briefly in Baltimore where he was a PhD. candidate in Biometrics/Statistics. We later both found ourselves in Hiroshima at the then Atomic Bomb Casualty Commission, where he was a statistician who became interested in genetics and genetical problems while I was a cytogeneticist, in sore need of his expertise in evaluating data. We proceeded for many years, at first in Japan where we collaborated on numerous studies, had fun doing so both then and later when back in the States, he at the University of Colorado Medical School while I was at Michigan, then Columbia. We did a lot of work together, were family friends, and all seemed good, for many years.

But, when I decided to leave Columbia, and later to go to Paris to do some work in which we were both interested, Phil seemed good with it at first, even endorsed the idea, came and visited. When I decided to stay in Europe, he seemed to take exception to that; and when I gave up the genetics and medicine altogether, well, that seemed to me to be more than he could tolerate. And so, we eventually after many years of camaraderie, gave up contact. And never resumed it.

My friend Stephen was an exception: Stephen and I go back to Boston Latin School days, where we were both stars in French. We continued our friendship on into Harvard. Steve would stay over occasionally in my Hollis Hall room – he commuted the first year from Roxbury – and he became active in the Harvard Radio Station (WHRB) as an announcer, which evolved into a lifelong parlaying of his formidable voice into an identity. Over the years we kept in touch, as he went on to the Harvard Business School, first as a student and later as a Professor (of Marketing). He was not really much involved in our very cohesive young men's B'nai Brith Haim Salomon Chapter of Alpha Zadik Alpha (AZA), standing on the periphery of it just a bit as a friend to many of us but especially to me.

Stephen and I had a disagreement when I decided to leave Columbia, because he so valued the academic world, still does even as an Emeritus Professor, while I valued more my freedom to move about and do whatever work I wished, wherever I wished. Despite that difference of opinion, he did not try to impose his view on me after having made his position clear to me: he felt I was making a mistake by leaving but once having spoken to the issue, he backed off and accepted my decision, understanding my craving to depart the hallowed halls of academia for points unchartered. But, to his credit Steve cared more about me as a brother than an academic co-believer. He and his wife Linda, a distinguished educator, visited us in Paris which they both love. Stephen and I, especially, have become yet closer on my return first from Paris, and now to Greater Boston.

In another way we differ: Stephen is a creature of consummate habit – 50 years a subscriber to the Boston Symphony Orchestra, for example; steadfast supporter of museums in and around Boston; and a lifelong active supporter of the Latin School Association and of Harvard College Alumni. He is, in that regard, what I could not be or do. And yet the ties are strong……

I believe, then, that friendship is to some degree like marriage: Hard to say why you can have a relationship with some over a lifetime, just as it is hard to define why you fall in love with the woman you fall in love with and make a commitment to one and not the other. Undoubtedly it is a matter of forming an emotional attachment that can withstand the many changes – marriage, relocations, progeny, career changes – that life inevitably involves. And friends at one stage of life are not necessarily friends at another.

Another kind of friendship exists, as it did for me and my fellow Alephs in the AZA: The brother in arms attachment, to the group that has one's loyalty. Might be the Marines. Might be the fan club of the Giants. Or often might be being a fellow alumnus of a college or grad school. Now this kind of brotherhood is not simply affection for the "guys" as a group and individually – it is a feeling of pride in the group per se. As Harvard was and will always be for me and the Class of '56ers, who faithfully gather for monthly luncheons at the Harvard Club of Boston to talk with one another about their lives, and their families, and whatever else is on their minds – the initial glue for us was the Harvard education, or the Boston Latin

School educational trauma and triumph, or the fun we had together as younger men; for others it might be the super bowl wins of the Giants or Patriots. But that glue in some such friendships is simply the initial group identity.

There were 25 or more AZAers originally linked in High School. Our closeness developed via interactions at weekly meetings, Saturday night parties, shared celebrations of Jewish festivals like Chanukah and Passover. We ran a fund-raising event for our yearly scholarship dance at the Totem Poll Dance Hall out in Newton, and played basketball games at which we were never much good.

While the Group dispersed after high school - though most of the guys went to Harvard - and scattered yet farther than Cambridge after college, a small core remained in contact, or at least resumed contact once settled down. But the still later-in-life coming together of the core Group of Eight was yet more of a miracle. With Sumner (aka Zummie), a special friend; Jerry D, another special friend; and Arnie, Marty, Paul, Donnie, Ray, and myself (aka then as Archie), there have been get-togethers in recent years in Paris, in Tuscany, in Southern California, in Cambridge, with wives accompanying us for up to a week or more at a time.

Of the Group of Eight we are now down to a Group of Seven, dear Paul having passed on because of Alzheimer's in 2016. The rest of us have made it into our 80's, in reasonably good health. The pivotal moment in the comings-together of our later years was the gathering in Paris, where the level of camaraderie was so very high - among the former Alephs and among their wives, too, somehow.

Thus, most of my friendships came from early–on relationships, with an occasional one from professional or social interactions in middle life. Robert G, of RKO Pictures, and I met in Paris in the 1990's and we two ex-pats became close friends. Our lunches of *foie de veau* at Café Luxembourg were special events.

I have often thought about the effects of my leaving Columbia and later of leaving the States not only on my family but on my colleagues. After a life of such intense involvement with them in the halls of academia – with all the involvements that implies and all the shared joys and pain we experienced – I simply, from their points of view simply, flew off to Paris and did not return for many years. I was as though dead to them, I suppose. I did keep in touch with those who mattered most, and I dutifully returned for an occasional Harvard Reunion. Fortunately the internet and email facilitated my communications; but basically, I no longer attended conferences in genetics; no longer had dinners or evenings out and about with colleagues during New York State Clinical Genetic gatherings and NIH Study Section meetings; no longer was a presence in my Genetics Clinic or my Laboratory at Columbia, or at Faculty Meetings. I allowed my membership in the Society of Human Genetics to lapse. And I recognized the likely myriad of hurt feelings and anguish I caused, the result, perhaps inevitable, of my departure from the States and the world of academic genetics.

For my part it has been as though my colleagues all remained alive, fixed in my mind as they were at the time of my leave-taking, never to age, never to die, though some of them obviously have. Maybe they too shall always see me as I was then. But truth is most have gone on to do good things and have not suffered unduly from my absence: FN, who ran my research labs at Michigan and Columbia moved out to Wyoming and Tennessee to go fishing, at which he was superb; FS left my diagnostic genetics lab at the Berkshire Medical Center, and became head of the Science Department at a local Massachusetts high school; KY took over my Genetics Clinic at Columbia; and ES, a particularly able graduate student who got her PhD with me at Michigan, went out to Colorado and has run the diagnostic DNA laboratory at the Medical Center there in Denver for many years. SRY, another PhD student of mine, has gone on to make a major contribution in genetics at the University of South Carolina. And Kyoo Wan Choi, my first graduate student, went on to become a distinguished Professor of Medicine at Seoul National University, where I had a marvelous visit with him years ago. Most of the others who were not a part of my inner circle of co-workers, were not people with whom I shared the daily event, but were friends from around the country and abroad, doubtless noted my absence with puzzlement and uncertainty.

But, I had to leave to become what I wished to become: something other than the doctor–scientist I dreamed of becoming in my youth. I dreamed new dreams as I got older and as time was running out. And so I had set off in my attempt to realize my new dreams. We have the right. No, we have the duty to do so. As Henry David Thoreau of Massachusetts wrote, “If a man does not keep pace with his companions, perhaps it is because he hears a different drummer. Let him step to the music he hears, however measured or far away."

PENSÉES III. On Politics

I was elected (2017) to the Gloucester Democratic City Committee, and represented Ward 4 at the State Convention in Worcester, where we approved, not surprisingly, in June 2017 a "Progressive Platform" for the Democratic Party of Massachusetts, including new and rent-controlled housing which Massachusetts desperately needs more of, as well as Government-controlled boutiques for the sale of marijuana. My entry into State Party politics took place when we lived a couple of years ago in the South End of Boston. I was then elected from Ward 4 in Boston, to the State Nominating Convention also held in Worcester. That year (2014) we nominated a full slate of Democratic candidates, from Governor and Lt. Governor on to Attorney General and State Treasurer, and our activism was rewarded, as often happens in the Bay State, with the election of almost all state-wide Democrats with the exception of a Republican Governor (Charlie Baker, a businessman from Swampscott). And I plan to go to the 2018 Massachusetts State Democratic Nominating Convention as an elected Delegate from Ward 1 in Gloucester.

My active interest in politics was fanned in 2012 when I worked in North Miami for the Obama Campaign, going door to door, soliciting votes on Obama's behalf. I have been concerned life-long about equality of the races, and that experience in the Obama campaign was seminal for me, a logical extension of my participation longer ago in the Martin Luther King, Jr. March on Washington during the Jack Kennedy era.

In my family as I grew up, as in most Jewish households in Dorchester, we were card-carrying Democrats, a graft which held most of us for our lifetimes. The values were those of the Democratic Party of Mr. Franklin Roosevelt and our intolerance, if we had any, was aimed at mean-spirited Republicans, and the Brahmins of Beacon Hill. At Harvard when Adlai E. Stevenson of Illinois came through in his campaign against Ike in 1952, I stood on the sidewalk on Mass. Ave and cheered my heart out for the man with the holes in his soles. In France I was largely party-neutral, had little interest in politics, France not really being my country and, anyway, I did not have the vote there.

So, I came honestly by a renewed interest in politics on my return from Paris. But, the Tennessee time had made it clear to me that the gap between the progressive liberals of the Blue States and the working class, often rural voters of the Red States, was not being bridged by the Democrats. That feeling has only increased in this the age of Trump because there is a clear opening for the Democrats but the Democratic leadership has made no strong efforts to fill it. We Democrats are same old, same old, both in terms of the programs and the people who serve as our voices in Washington.

For that reason, along with a certain cynicism born of age, I now turn the "progressive" MSNBC Rachel Maddow Show off, and curtail my hours with CNN's Wolf Blitzer to a precious few. I do try to exclude politics from my writings, though I am obviously not entirely successful at that.

Pensées IV. On Family

I grew up in the warmth of The Holidays - the Jewish Holidays, of *Pesach* (the Exodus from Egypt), *Rosh Hashonah* (the Jewish New Year), *Yom Kippur* (the Day of Atonement), *Sukkot* (the Feast of Tabernacles), and *Chanukah* (the Feast of Lights). Each Holy Day had its customs and while I often rebelled as I got older against the rituals and prescribed modes of behavior surrounding them, I bathed in them during my earlier years, and was held by them. And by those who celebrated them with me.

As I have traveled the world doing my thing I have also come to enjoy the holidays of others. The European, especially French, way of celebrating Christmas, for example, is filled with customs foreign to a Dorchester guy: In France Christmas Eve began for us at 9 or 10pm, with the obligatory Taittinger or Veuve Clicquot Champagne followed by plates of smoked salmon on blinis, then oysters, and claw-less lobsters from Brittany; then on to my favorite *foie gras* with sauterne. Usually a goose or pheasant served to cap the dinner - I still do the goose here in the U.S. but on Christmas Day - and the meal invariably ended there in Paris with a *Bûche de Noel*, a very elegant, chocolated, Yule Log. Christmas gifts in most French homes are opened on Christmas Eve, but we held to Christmas morning to exchange gifts.

Family time was ceded in France to friends with whom to celebrate New Year's Eve, with parties and drinking, as here in the United States.

In Japan, in contrast, Christmas was party time, a great revelry in the local bars. The family gathering in Japan is at New Year's and for some days beyond. The wonderful

Buddhist ringing of temple bells in Japan on New Year's Eve is unforgettable: The largest bell in Japan – 74 tons - is the bronze bell at *Chionin* in the gorgeous *Higashiyama* (Eastern) Hills of Kyoto, and on New Year's Eve the custom is for 17 Buddhist monks to start swinging a five-meter suspended wooden log at the bell to elicit a deep, bass-like bong sound. The priests of Chionin – a temple built in the 13th century – strike the bell multiple times before midnight, but just once after midnight, to eliminate (by Buddhist calculation) the 108 mortal sins to which humanity is subject. The sound of the 108th strike, the one that rings in the New Year, is heard by neighboring temples and the monks of those local temples repeat the 108th blow of Chionin. In this way the sound of the bell is transmitted, ripple-like, up and down the archipelago and people await the tolling of the bell in their neighborhoods to recognize the start of the New Year. The sound would arrive each year in Hiroshima at about 12:40 a.m. and only after that would I go to sleep. Each year there I waited along with the entire nation to hear the last gasp of the bell.

(Note: The Chionin Temple serves as the Headquarters of a 13th century Buddhist Sect and this annual cleansing of our souls of sin allows us to be reborn in Paradise after death. Much as the Day of Atonement does in Judaism).

PENSÉES V. On Serious Aging

I am a serious fan/reader of the daily Obituary column whether online or in print, in the Boston Globe or the New York Times – it is not an odd pre-occupation for a gentleman of 84, though admittedly I have been such a reader for years now. How else, beside the Obits and word of mouth - which can take a very long time to reach one, especially in a smallish seaside town on the North Shore of Massachusetts - can I keep up with the passing of my dear friends, distant relatives and former colleagues? Anyway, I read them almost daily so as to keep up.

At the very beginning of 2018, 98 deaths with verifiable ages were reported in the Obituary column of the Boston Globe. Of these 98 deaths, 39 persons were under age 80; 34 were between 80 and 89; and 25 were above 90. Now, this is a small sample, taken over a very few days, but national statistics, I am told, would suggest the same things: First, and most important to me and my friends of Haym Salomon AZA and to my Harvard Classmates (1956), having reached at least 80, we have a better than 42 percent chance of living to 90 or beyond – a comforting statistic.

Then again, this is Boston, and thus a reasonably well-educated and well-heeled population, suggesting good quality medical care with less smoking and fewer no-nos (obesity, for example) than in some communities – Gatlinburg,Tennessee, for example. I recognize that weight, smoking history, high blood pressure, pre-existing conditions all, will play a role in one's age at death. But if 60 percent of our population broadly speaking will live to 80 and beyond, it suggests that we ought to prepare. Especially women who make up over 50 percent of the surviving older population.

It used to be that people worked until 65, when their Social Security kicked in, and then they "retired". Looked at critically, one may ask, retired to what? Babysitting the grandkids? Playing golf? Doing a little volunteer work at the local hospital? Many did these things and were content, but many also dropped dead before they could get into the swing of the "Golden Years", retirement itself being a killer at times. (My dear friend RT retired at 70 from his insurance business, and I asked him some months later how it was going. He said fine except his wife was having trouble: when they got married she signed on for two meals a day at retirement but not three!)

One of the main theses which drove the writing of this book was that we can prepare, prepare to live a second kind of life in our later years, different in some important ways from our first, if we wish it to be. While my life's voyage has been circuitous, from one career to another, from one country to another, and from one city or country place to another - as the preceding pages testify - the voyage has been largely a pleasure and often a downright joy. The beginnings in Boston were not "easy" by dint of my parents' divorce and our tight economic straits; but those years with my education served as the foundation for what was to come. I had early-on a warm family life, wrapped in a Jewish community that afforded me friends for a lifetime. I made friends in high school and college who have remained a vital part of my life. True, there were some from whom I parted - some whose death I have mourned, some I have separated from voluntarily, occasionally with bitterness - but as the years have passed, I have become grateful for the family and friends who remain standing by my side.

I am fortunate to have found my soulmate some 36 plus years ago, someone with whom I have shared in such depth the evolution of my life. And I have been blessed to have been able at the same time to hold my children close while enabling their own individualities to be expressed.

To Conclude, a minimally modified verse from Leonard Cohen:

> I did my best, it wasn't much
> I've told the truth, I didn't come to fool you,
> I'll stand before the Lord
> With nothing on my tongue but "Hallelujah."

Made in the USA
Columbia, SC
15 November 2018